UK Tower 2-Basket Air Fryer Cookbook 2024

1800 Days Healthy and Delicious Air Fryer Recipes for Beginners to Master Your Smart Tower Dual Zone Air Fryer

Mary P. Bosarge

Copyright© 2023 By Mary P. Bosarge
All Rights Reserved

This book is copyright protected. It is only for personal use.
You cannot amend, distribute, sell, use,
quote or paraphrase any part of the content within this book,
without the consent of the author or publisher.
Under no circumstances will any blame or
legal responsibility be held against the publisher,
or author, for any damages, reparation,
or monetary loss due to the information contained within this book,
either directly or indirectly.

Disclaimer Notice:
Please note the information contained within this
document is for educational and entertainment purposes only.
All effort has been executed to present accurate,
up to date, reliable, complete information.
No warranties of any kind are declared or implied.
Readers acknowledge that the author is not engaged
in the rendering of legal,
financial, medical or professional advice.
The content within this book has been derived from various sources.
Please consult a licensed professional before attempting any
techniques outlined in this book.
By reading this document,
the reader agrees that under no circumstances is the
author responsible for any losses,
direct or indirect,
that are incurred as a result of the use of the
information contained within this document, including,
but not limited to, errors, omissions, or inaccuracies.

Contents

Introduction 1
   What is the Tower Dual Basket Air Fryer? 1
   The Benefits and the Features of the Tower Dual Basket Air Fryer 2
   How to Use the Tower Dual Basket Air Fryer? (Tips for Cooking Success) ... 2
   How to Clean the Tower Dual Basket Air Fryer? 3
   FAQs About the Tower Dual Basket Air Fryer 4

Chapter 1: Breakfast Recipes 6
   Crispy Full English Breakfast 6
   Perfectly Poached Egg on Avocado Toast 6
   Air-Fried Mushroom and Spinach Omelette 6
   Fluffy Blueberry Pancakes 6
   Smoked Salmon and Cream Cheese Bagels 7
   Veggie Breakfast Hash with Halloumi 7
   English Muffin Breakfast Pizzas 7
   Air-Fried Sausage and Hash Brown Casserole 8
   Healthy Banana Walnut Muffins 8
   Spinach and Feta Breakfast Pastries 8
   Baked Breakfast Energy Bites 8
   Air-Fried Bubble and Squeak Patties 9
   Cheesy Bacon and Tomato Breakfast Quesadillas 9
   Breakfast Burrito Bowls with Black Beans and Avocado 10
   Air-Fried Scotch Eggs with Mustard Sauce 10
   Cinnamon Swirl French Toast Sticks 10
   Breakfast Stuffed Peppers with Eggs and Spinach 10
   Chocolate Chip Courgette Muffins 11
   Vegan Breakfast Tacos with Tofu Scramble 11
   Air-Fried Crumpets with Butter and Jam 11

Chapter 2: Snack Recipes 12
   Crispy Garlic Parmesan Potato Wedges 12
   Air-Fried Mini Corn Dogs with Mustard Dip 12
   Sweet and Spicy Air-Fried Chickpeas 12
   Cheese and Bacon Stuffed Mushrooms 12
   Crunchy Air-Fried Pickles with Ranch Dip 13
   Air-Fried Mozzarella Sticks with Marinara Sauce 13

Sticky Honey Mustard Chicken Wings 13
Spinach and Artichoke Stuffed Wontons..14
Air-Fried Vegetable Spring Rolls 14
Crispy Coconut Shrimp with Mango Dipping Sauce 14
Spiced Sweet Potato Fries with Chipotle Aioli 15
Buffalo Cauliflower Bites with Blue Cheese Dip 15
Air-Fried Jalapeño Poppers with Cream Cheese Filling..16
Mediterranean Stuffed Peppers 16
Caprese Skewers with Balsamic Glaze 16
Panko-Crusted Fish Tacos with Lime Crema 17
Mini Beef and Mushroom Wellingtons 17
Air-Fried Falafel with Tahini Sauce 17
Crispy Polenta Fries with Marinara Dip 18
Raspberry and Nutella Wonton Purses 18

Chapter 3: Lunch Recipes 19

Crispy Chicken Sandwich with Coleslaw 19
Air-Fried Fish and Chips with Tartar Sauce 19
Veggie-Stuffed Air-Fried Calzone 19
Air Fryer Pesto Chicken Pasta Salad 20
Air-Fried Falafel Wrap with Hummus 20
BBQ Pulled Pork Sliders 21
Crispy Halloumi and Vegetable Skewers 21
Mushroom and Spinach Stuffed Chicken Breast 21
Air-Fried Sweet Potato and Chickpea Patties..21
Spicy Shrimp Tacos with coriander Lime Slaw 22
Mediterranean Quinoa Salad with Feta 22
Air-Fried Aubergine Parmesan 23
Classic BLT Sandwich with Avocado 23
Lemon Herb Air-Fried Salmon 23
Teriyaki Tofu Stir Fry with Vegetables 24
Spinach and Feta Stuffed Portobello Mushrooms 24
Air-Fried Prawn and Mango Salad 24
Caprese Panini with Balsamic Glaze 25
Crispy Pork Schnitzel with Lemon Butter Sauce 25
Air-Fried Vegetable and Chickpea Fritters 25

Chapter 4: Dinner Recipes 26

Crispy Air-Fried Chicken Thighs with Herbs..26

Air-Fried Lamb Chops with Mint Sauce...26
Vegetable and Chickpea Air-Fried Curry 26
Teriyaki Salmon with Stir-Fried Vegetables 26
Air-Fried Beef and Vegetable Stir Fry 27
Honey Garlic Air-Fried Pork Tenderloin 27
Mediterranean Air-Fried Sea Bass 27
Air-Fried Pesto and Mozzarella Stuffed Chicken 27
Crispy Coconut-Crusted Tofu with Sweet Chilli Sauce 28
Air-Fried Sausages with Onion Gravy 28
Lemon Herb Air-Fried Cod Fillets 28
Air-Fried Vegetable and Paneer Skewers 28
Crispy Air-Fried Duck Breast with Orange Glaze 29
Air-Fried Beef and Mushroom Pie 29
Stuffed Peppers with Quinoa and Cheese 29
Air-Fried Butter Chicken with Naan Bread 30
Air-Fried BBQ Pork Ribs 30
Crispy Air-Fried Falafel Platter 30
Air-Fried Shrimp Scampi with Linguine 31
Air-Fried Vegetable and Lentil Curry..31

Chapter 5: Vegetable and Vegetarian Recipes 32

Crispy Air-Fried Vegetable Spring Rolls 32
Stuffed Portobello Mushrooms with Spinach and Feta 32
Air-Fried Sweet Potato Wedges with Rosemary...32
Spicy Air-Fried Cauliflower Bites 32
Crispy Halloumi Fries with Yoghurt Dip 33
Air-Fried Mediterranean Stuffed Peppers 33
Air-Fried Veggie Burger Patties 33
Panko-Crusted Air-Fried Courgette Chips 34
Air-Fried Asparagus Spears with Lemon Zest 34
Stuffed Butternut Squash with Quinoa and Cranberries...34
Air-Fried Brussels Sprouts with Balsamic Glaze 35
Air-Fried Vegetable Tempura with Dipping Sauce...35
Crispy Air-Fried Tofu Nuggets 35
Air-Fried Ratatouille with Herbs de Provence 35
Sweet and Spicy Air-Fried Carrots 36
Air-Fried Chickpea and Spinach Falafel..36
Air-Fried Stuffed Mushrooms with Herbs 36
Crispy Air-Fried Aubergine Slices 37

Air-Fried Sesame-Ginger Broccoli Florets 37
Air-Fried Veggie Kebabs with Tzatziki Sauce 37

Chapter 6: Sides and Appetisers Recipes 38

Crispy Air-Fried Potato Skins with Cheddar and Bacon 38
Air-Fried Mac and Cheese Bites with Sriracha Mayo 38
Parmesan and Garlic Air-Fried Green Beans 38
Panko-Crusted Air-Fried Mushrooms with Aioli 39
Spicy Sweet Potato Fries with Chipotle Dip 39
Air-Fried Halloumi and Tomato Skewers 39
Crispy Air-Fried Onion Rings with Tangy Dip 40
Air-Fried Cornbread Muffins with Honey Butter 40
Air-Fried Jalapeño Poppers with Creamy Ranch 40
Crispy Air-Fried Polenta Fries with Marinara 41
Stuffed Mini Peppers with Cream Cheese and Herbs 41
Air-Fried Pesto Potato Wedges 41
Air-Fried Pickle Spears with Dill Dip...42
Crispy Air-Fried Avocado Fries with Lime Dip 42
Air-Fried Stuffed Jalapeños with Bacon and Cheese 42
Garlic Herb Air-Fried Breaded Mushrooms 43
Air-Fried Halloumi Fritters with Sweet Chilli Sauce 43
Crispy Air-Fried Artichoke Hearts with Lemon Aioli 43
Air-Fried Sweet Corn Fritters with Yoghurt Dip 44
Crispy Air-Fried Asparagus Spears with Lemon Zest 44

Chapter 7: Hearty Stew Recipes 45

Air-Fried Hearty Beef and Ale Stew 45
Air-Fried Traditional Lamb and Vegetable Stew 45
Air-Fried Rich Guinness Beef Stew 45
Air-Fried Classic Chicken and Mushroom Stew 46
Air-Fried Homely Vegetable and Barley Stew 46
Smoky Sausage and Bean Stew 47
Rustic Pork and Cider Stew 47
Fragrant Thai Green Curry Stew...47
Hearty Lentil and Vegetable Stew 48
Spicy Chickpea and Spinach Stew 48
Creamy Seafood Chowder 48
Moroccan-inspired Lamb and Apricot Stew 49
Savoury Venison and Red Wine Stew 49

Cosy Potato and Leek Soup 49
Irish Lamb and Guinness Stew 50
Tuscan-inspired Tomato and Bread Stew 50
Spiced Pumpkin and Lentil Stew 50
Spanish Chorizo and Chickpea Stew 51
Hearty Beef and Vegetable Casserole 51
Warm and Comforting Minestrone Stew 51

Chapter 8: Fish and Seafood Recipes 52

Crispy Beer-Battered Fish and Chips 52
Air-Fried Lemon Garlic Salmon Fillets 52
Spicy Cajun Shrimp Skewers 52
Crispy Breaded Haddock Fillets 53
Garlic Butter Prawns with Herbs 53
Air-Fried Fish Tacos with Lime Crema 53
Sesame-Crusted Tuna Steaks 54
Air-Fried Coconut Shrimp with Mango Dipping Sauce 54
Classic Fish Pie with a Twist 54
Teriyaki Glazed Salmon with Sesame Seeds 55
Air-Fried Lemon Herb Scallops 55
Pesto Crusted Sea Bass Fillets 55
Crispy Calamari Rings with Aioli Dip 56
Lemon Dill Air-Fried Cod Fillets 56
Spicy Sriracha Salmon Burgers 56
Crispy Fish Fingers with Tartar Sauce 57
Garlic Butter Lobster Tails 57
Blackened Cajun Catfish Fillets 58
Smoked Paprika Prawns with Aioli 58
Mediterranean Grilled Swordfish Steaks 58

Chapter 9: Beef, Pork and Lamb Recipes 59

Succulent Air-Fried Beef Sirloin Steak 59
Crispy Pork Belly with Apple Compote 59
Spicy BBQ Pulled Pork Sliders 59
Air-Fried Lamb Chops with Mint Glaze 60
Classic Beef and Guinness Pie 60
Sticky Teriyaki Pork Tenderloin 61
Fragrant Rosemary Lamb Kebabs 61
Air-Fried Beef Stir-Fry with Vegetables 61

Tangy Balsamic Glazed Pork Ribs 61
Air-Fried Moroccan Lamb Meatballs 62
Crispy Pork Schnitzel with Lemon Butter 62
Spicy Korean BBQ Beef Skewers 62
Air-Fried Garlic Rosemary Lamb Chops 63
Honey Mustard Glazed Pork Loin 63
Fragrant Ginger Beef Stir Fry..63
Savoury Lamb and Mushroom Pie 64
Air-Fried Pork and Leek Dumplings 64
Beef and Mushroom Stuffed Peppers 64
Air-Fried Lamb Gyros with Tzatziki 65
Pork and Sage Sausage Rolls 65

Chapter 10: Sweet Treats and Dessert Recipes 66

Air-Fried Apple Fritters with Cinnamon Sugar 66
Crispy Mini Jam Doughnuts 66
Decadent Chocolate Lava Cake 66
Sticky Toffee Pudding Bites 67
Banana Bread 67
Classic Victoria Sponge Cake...68
Zesty Lemon Curd Tarts 68
Air-Fried Raspberry Cheesecake Bites 68
Cinnamon Sugar Churros with Chocolate Sauce 69
Blueberry and Cream Cheese Air-Fried Pastry 69
Crispy Custard-Filled Eclairs 70
Air-Fried Sticky Caramel Pudding 70
Raspberry and Almond Frangipane Tartlets 71
Air-Fried Mango Coconut Spring Rolls 71
Mini Pavlovas with Fresh Berries 71
Air-Fried Chocolate Orange Profiteroles 72
Spiced Apple and Walnut Turnovers 72
Air-Fried Chocolate Hazelnut Calzones 72
Black Forest Cherry and Chocolate Parfait 73
Crispy Air-Fried Pineapple Fritters..73

Introduction

Welcome to the culinary world of guilt-free indulgence! I am delighted to introduce you to my "UK Tower 2-Basket Air Fryer Cookbook," your passport to a healthier, happier, and utterly delicious cooking experience. In the delightful pages that follow, you'll embark on a gastronomic journey that marries the rich tapestry of British cuisine with the innovative wonders of air frying.

Prepare to be amazed as we explore the vast possibilities of your Tower 2-Basket Air Fryer, transforming ordinary ingredients into extraordinary delights. Whether you're a seasoned home chef or a novice in the kitchen, this cookbook is your trusted companion, inspiring you to create mouthwatering dishes that are as wholesome as they are flavoursome.

With a sprinkle of creativity and a dash of enthusiasm, we'll dive into classic recipes, giving them a modern twist while retaining the authentic tastes you know and love. From crispy fish and chips to perfectly roasted vegetables, get ready to savour the irresistible aroma of your favourite British meals, all made with a healthier touch.

But this cookbook is more than just a collection of recipes; it's a celebration of your culinary adventures. Each page is infused with encouragement, urging you to explore, experiment, and, most importantly, enjoy the process. So, don your apron, preheat your Tower Air Fryer, and let's embark on a cooking expedition filled with joy, flavour, and wholesome goodness.

What is the Tower Dual Basket Air Fryer?

Allow me to introduce you to the marvel that is the Tower Dual Basket Air Fryer! Picture this: a kitchen appliance that combines innovation and simplicity in the most delightful way possible. The Tower Dual Basket Air Fryer is your ticket to healthier, hassle-free cooking, and it's about to revolutionise the way you approach your meals.

Imagine crispy, golden delights emerging from the depths of this sleek machine, minus the excessive oil and guilt. With not one, but two spacious baskets, you have the power to multitask like a culinary wizard. It means you can indulge in the joy of frying without drowning your food in unhealthy fats. Instead, hot air circulates around your ingredients, ensuring they're cooked to perfection with that ideal crunch, all while retaining their natural goodness. The intuitive controls of the Tower Dual Basket Air Fryer put the power firmly in your hands. Want to roast some veggies while air frying your favourite snacks? Easy. Craving for guilt-free fried chicken? You got it. The adjustable temperature and timer settings make experimenting with recipes a breeze, ensuring every dish is cooked just the way you like it.

Plus, cleaning up is a cinch! The removable,

dishwasher-safe parts mean you can bid farewell to the tedious scrubbing usually associated with traditional cooking methods.

In essence, the Tower Dual Basket Air Fryer isn't just a kitchen gadget; it's a game-changer. It's your culinary sidekick, your ticket to healthier indulgence, and your secret ingredient for creating mouthwatering dishes without the fuss. So buckle up, because your cooking adventure is about to take a delicious, guilt-free turn!

The Benefits and the Features of the Tower Dual Basket Air Fryer

Let's delve into the treasure trove of benefits and features that the Tower Dual Basket Air Fryer brings to your kitchen kingdom. Get ready to be amazed because this innovative wonder isn't just another kitchen gadget – it's a culinary game-changer designed with your convenience and health in mind.

Double the Delight
The Tower Dual Basket Air Fryer features not one, but two spacious baskets, allowing you to cook multiple dishes simultaneously. It's a multitasker's dream come true, perfect for busy cooks who want to whip up a feast without the stress.

Healthy Indulgence
Say goodbye to excessive oil without sacrificing taste! This air fryer uses hot air circulation to cook your favourite meals, ensuring they're crispy and delightful while significantly reducing unhealthy fats. It's guilt-free indulgence at its finest.

Precision Cooking
Take control with adjustable temperature and timer settings. Whether you're searing, baking, or roasting, the Tower Dual Basket Air Fryer offers precision at your fingertips, guaranteeing each dish is cooked to perfection.

Effortless Cleaning
No more dreading the post-cooking cleanup. The removable, dishwasher-safe parts make tidying up a breeze, allowing you to enjoy your culinary creations without worrying about the mess.

Space-Saving Design
Despite its double-basket capacity, the Tower Dual Basket Air Fryer boasts a sleek and compact design, saving precious countertop space in your kitchen. It's a powerhouse that fits seamlessly into your culinary haven.

Endless Culinary Adventures
From crispy fries to succulent grilled vegetables, this air fryer unlocks a world of culinary possibilities. It's not just an appliance; it's an invitation to explore, experiment, and create mouthwatering masterpieces right in your own home.

So there you have it – the Tower Dual Basket Air Fryer isn't just a kitchen appliance; it's a revolutionary tool designed to elevate your cooking experience. Get ready to embark on a journey of healthier, tastier, and more convenient meals. Your kitchen will never be the same again!

How to Use the Tower Dual Basket Air Fryer? (Tips for Cooking Success)

Let's dive into the nitty-gritty of mastering your Tower Dual Basket Air Fryer. Buckle up, because by the end of this, you'll be a pro at using this culinary marvel.

Step 1: Familiarise Yourself with Your Air Fryer
Before you start your air frying adventure, get to know your Tower Dual Basket Air Fryer inside out. Read the user manual carefully, acquaint yourself with the control panel, and understand the functions of each button. It's like getting to know the controls of a new car – familiarity leads to confidence.

Step 2: Preheat Like a Pro
Preheating is key to achieving that perfect, crispy texture. Set your air fryer to the desired temperature (typically between 350°F to 400°F or 175°C to 200°C) and let it preheat for a few minutes. Preheating ensures that your food starts cooking the moment it hits the basket, giving you that delightful crunch.

Step 3: Prep Your Ingredients
While your air fryer is preheating, prep your ingredients. Pat dry any moisture from your food, as excess moisture can hinder the crisping process. If you're working with items like potatoes, a light coating of oil can enhance the crunch factor.

Step 4: Load the Baskets with Care
One of the fantastic features of the Tower Dual Basket Air Fryer is its ability to cook two different dishes simultaneously. Place the food items evenly in the baskets, ensuring there's some space between them for proper air circulation. Don't overcrowd – allowing the hot air to flow around your food ensures even cooking.

Step 5: Set the Time and Temperature
Refer to the recipe or cooking guidelines for the specific time and temperature settings. Adjust the temperature and timer using the user-friendly controls on your air fryer. Keep an eye on your food while it cooks – cooking times might vary based on the quantity and thickness of your ingredients.

Step 6: Shake and Check
For an even crisp, pause the air fryer halfway through the cooking time. Carefully shake the baskets to toss the food inside. This step ensures that all sides of your food are exposed to the hot air, promoting uniform cooking.

Step 7: Enjoy Your Culinary Masterpiece
Once the timer beeps, your perfectly air-fried delights are ready to be savoured! Carefully remove the baskets (they'll be hot, so use oven mitts) and let your creations cool for a minute before indulging.

Step 8: Cleaning Up
After your culinary adventure, cleaning up is a breeze. Remove the baskets and any other

detachable parts, then wash them with warm, soapy water. Better yet, many parts are dishwasher-safe, making cleanup even more convenient.

There you have it – your comprehensive guide to using the Tower Dual Basket Air Fryer like a seasoned chef. With a little practice and a lot of enthusiasm, you'll be whipping up delicious, healthier meals in no time. Happy air frying!

How to Clean the Tower Dual Basket Air Fryer?

Maintaining the cleanliness of your Tower Dual Basket Air Fryer ensures its optimal performance and longevity. Here's your complete guide to keeping your kitchen companion spick and span:

Step 1: Safety First
Before you dive into cleaning, unplug your Tower Dual Basket Air Fryer and make sure it's completely cooled down. Safety is paramount in the cleaning process.

Step 2: Disassemble Carefully
Begin by removing the baskets, trays, and any other detachable components. Check your user manual to identify which parts are dishwasher-safe. Typically, the baskets and trays are dishwasher-friendly, making cleanup a breeze.

Step 3: Hand Wash Non-Dishwasher-Safe Parts
For parts that aren't dishwasher-safe, like the heating element and the exterior of the air fryer, use a damp cloth or sponge with warm, soapy water to wipe away any grease or residue. Be gentle and avoid abrasive cleaners, as they might damage the non-stick coating.

Step 4: Tackle Stubborn Stains
For stubborn stains or residue inside the baskets or trays, a mixture of baking soda and water can work wonders. Create a paste and gently scrub the affected areas. Rinse thoroughly afterwards to ensure no residue remains.

Step 5: Clean the Exterior
Wipe down the exterior of your air fryer with a damp cloth. If there are persistent stains, a mild all-purpose kitchen cleaner can be used. Remember, never spray cleaning products directly onto the air fryer – apply them to your cleaning cloth instead.

Step 6: Addressing Odours
If your air fryer has picked up odours from previous cooking sessions, a simple solution is to place a bowl of equal parts water and white vinegar inside the fryer basket. Run the air fryer at a low temperature for a few minutes. The vinegar helps neutralise odours, leaving your air fryer smelling fresh.

Step 7: Reassemble and Store
Once all parts are clean and dry, reassemble your Tower Dual Basket Air Fryer. Ensure everything is properly fitted before storing it away. Store your air fryer in a cool, dry place, ready for your next culinary adventure.

Step 8: Regular Maintenance
To maintain your air fryer's performance, it's advisable to clean it after every use. Prompt cleaning prevents buildup and ensures that your air fryer continues to produce perfectly cooked, delicious meals.

And there you have it – a thorough guide to keeping your Tower Dual Basket Air Fryer in pristine condition. Regular cleaning not only preserves its functionality but also guarantees that each meal you prepare is as delectable as the last.

FAQs About the Tower Dual Basket Air Fryer

Let's answer some of your most frequently asked questions about the Tower Dual Basket Air Fryer!

Can I cook different foods simultaneously in the two baskets of the Tower Dual Basket Air Fryer?
Absolutely! One of the fantastic features of the Tower Dual Basket Air Fryer is its ability to cook different foods simultaneously. The two baskets allow you to prepare separate dishes without any flavour mingling, making your cooking process more efficient and versatile.

Is it necessary to preheat the air fryer before cooking?
Yes, preheating is essential for achieving that perfect, crispy texture. Preheating your Tower Dual Basket Air Fryer for a few minutes at the desired temperature ensures that your food starts cooking instantly when you put it in, resulting in evenly cooked and delicious meals.

How do I clean the baskets and trays of the air fryer?
The baskets and trays of your Tower Dual Basket Air Fryer are typically dishwasher-safe. You can simply remove them after use and wash them in warm, soapy water or put them in the dishwasher. For stubborn stains, a mixture of baking soda and water can be used as a gentle scrubbing agent.

Can I use parchment paper or aluminium foil in the baskets?
Yes, you can use parchment paper or aluminium foil in the baskets of your air fryer. However, make sure to trim the paper or foil so that it doesn't obstruct the air circulation. This allows your food to cook evenly while still enjoying the benefits of easy cleanup.

What is the maximum cooking temperature of the Tower Dual Basket Air Fryer?
The Tower Dual Basket Air Fryer typically reaches a maximum temperature of around 400°F or 200°C. This high-temperature range gives you the flexibility to cook a wide variety of foods, from crispy fries to succulent meats and vegetables.

Can I adjust the cooking time and temperature during the cooking process?
Yes, you can easily adjust both the cooking time and temperature while using your Tower Dual Basket Air Fryer. The intuitive control panel allows you to tweak these settings according to your recipe's requirements, ensuring precise cooking and perfect results.

Is it normal to hear a fan noise during operation?
Yes, it is perfectly normal to hear a fan noise while the Tower Dual Basket Air Fryer is in operation. The fan is responsible for circulating the hot air, ensuring even cooking. The noise level is generally low and indicates that your air fryer is functioning as it should.

Can I cook frozen foods directly in the air fryer without thawing?
Yes, you can cook frozen foods directly in the Tower Dual Basket Air Fryer without thawing. In fact, air fryers are excellent for cooking frozen foods as they result in a crispy texture without the need for excessive oil. Just adjust the cooking time and temperature according to the frozen food packaging instructions for delicious, hassle-free meals.

As we conclude this warm culinary embrace, I invite you to embark on a journey that's not just about cooking but about creating delightful memories in your kitchen. The "UK Tower 2-Basket Air Fryer Cookbook" is more than a collection of recipes; it's a gateway to healthier, flavourful meals that celebrate the joy of food without the guilt.

Armed with your Tower Dual Basket Air Fryer and this treasure trove of recipes, you are now equipped to transform ordinary ingredients into extraordinary culinary masterpieces. So, what are you waiting for? Dive into the pages that follow, let your taste buds dance with excitement, and bring the delectable aromas of these recipes to life in your very own kitchen.

I encourage you to explore, experiment, and, most importantly, enjoy the process. Each recipe is a canvas waiting for your personal touch, a canvas that promises a symphony of flavours and a feast for the senses. So turn the page, pick a recipe that tantalises your taste buds, and let the adventure begin.

Happy cooking, dear reader! Let's make every meal a celebration. Your culinary adventure starts now – turn the page and let the magic unfold!

Chapter 1: Breakfast Recipes

Crispy Full English Breakfast

Serves: 2 / Prep time: 15 minutes / Cook time: 20 minutes

Ingredients:
- 300g back bacon rashers
- 200g Cumberland sausages
- 200g black pudding slices
- 300g cherry tomatoes, halved
- 200g button mushrooms, halved
- 4 large eggs • 400g hash brown potatoes
- 60ml vegetable oil
- Salt and black pepper, to taste
- Fresh parsley, chopped, for garnish

Preparation instructions:
1. Preheat your Air Fryer to 200°C for 5 minutes.
2. In one basket, arrange bacon, sausages, black pudding, cherry tomatoes, and mushrooms.
3. In the other basket, place hash brown potatoes, drizzle with vegetable oil, and season with salt and black pepper.
4. Air fry both baskets at 200°C for 20 minutes or until the bacon is crispy, sausages are cooked through, and the hash browns are golden brown.
5. While the breakfast items are air frying, prepare poached eggs separately on the stove.
6. Serve the crispy Full English breakfast with poached eggs on the side, garnished with fresh parsley.

Perfectly Poached Egg on Avocado Toast

Serves: 2 / Prep time: 10 minutes / Cook time: 5 minutes

Ingredients:
- 2 large eggs • 2 slices of wholegrain bread
- 1 ripe avocado, mashed • 1 tbsp lemon juice
- Salt and black pepper, to taste
- Fresh chives, chopped, for garnish

Preparation instructions:
1. Preheat your Air Fryer to 180°C for 5 minutes.
2. While the Air Fryer is heating, prepare mashed avocado by mixing it with lemon juice, salt, and black pepper.
3. Toast the bread slices in one basket at 180°C for 3 minutes or until golden brown.
4. In the other basket, carefully crack the eggs and air fry at 180°C for 5 minutes or until the whites are set but the yolks are still runny.
5. Spread mashed avocado evenly over the toasted bread slices.
6. Gently place the perfectly poached eggs on top of the avocado toast and garnish with fresh chives before serving.

Air-Fried Mushroom and Spinach Omelette

Serves: 2 / Prep time: 10 minutes / Cook time: 10 minutes

Ingredients:
- 200g button mushrooms, sliced
- 100g fresh spinach leaves
- 4 large eggs • 60ml whole milk
- 50g cheddar cheese, grated
- 1 tbsp butter • Salt and black pepper, to taste
- Fresh parsley, chopped, for garnish

Preparation instructions:
1. Preheat your Air Fryer to 180°C for 5 minutes.
2. In a non-stick pan, sauté sliced mushrooms in butter until tender, then add fresh spinach and cook until wilted.
3. In a bowl, whisk together eggs, whole milk, grated cheddar cheese, salt, and black pepper.
4. Pour the egg mixture over the mushrooms and spinach in the pan.
5. Cook the omelette on the stovetop until the edges are set.
6. Transfer the pan to the Air Fryer and airfryer at 180°C for 5 minutes or until the omelette is fully set and slightly golden on top.
7. Garnish with fresh parsley before serving.

Fluffy Blueberry Pancakes

Serves: 4 / Prep time: 10 minutes / Cook time: 15 minutes

Ingredients:
- 200g all-purpose flour
- 2 tbsp sugar
- 1 tbsp baking powder
- 1/2 tsp salt
- 240 ml whole milk
- 2 large eggs
- 1 tbsp vegetable oil
- 150g fresh blueberries
- Butter, for serving
- Maple syrup, for serving

Preparation instructions:
1. In a bowl, whisk together flour, sugar, baking powder, and salt.
2. In another bowl, whisk together milk, eggs, and vegetable oil.
3. Pour the wet ingredients into the dry ingredients and stir until just combined. Gently fold in the fresh blueberries.
4. Preheat your Air Fryer to 180°C for 5 minutes.
5. Grease the Air Fryer basket with a little oil.
6. Spoon the pancake batter into the basket to form small rounds.
7. Air fry at 180°C for 7-8 minutes on each side or until the pancakes are puffed and golden.
8. Serve the fluffy blueberry pancakes with butter and maple syrup.

Smoked Salmon and Cream Cheese Bagels

Serves: 2 / Prep time: 10 minutes / Cook time: 5 minutes

Ingredients:
- 2 wholegrain bagels, halved
- 150g smoked salmon slices
- 100g cream cheese
- Capers, for garnish
- 1 small red onion, thinly sliced
- Fresh dill, chopped, for garnish
- Lemon wedges, for serving

Preparation instructions:
1. Preheat your Air Fryer to 180°C for 5 minutes.
2. While the Air Fryer is heating, spread cream cheese evenly over the cut sides of the bagels.
3. Place smoked salmon slices on the bottom halves of the bagels and top with thinly sliced red onion.
4. Assemble the bagels and air fry at 180°C for 5 minutes or until they are warm and slightly crispy.
5. Garnish with capers and fresh dill.
6. Serve the smoked salmon and cream cheese bagels with lemon wedges on the side.

Veggie Breakfast Hash with Halloumi

Serves: 4 / Prep time: 15 minutes / Cook time: 20 minutes

Ingredients:
- 500g diced potatoes
- 2 tbsp olive oil
- 200g halloumi cheese, cubed
- 1 red bell pepper, chopped
- 1 yellow bell pepper, chopped
- 1 red onion, finely chopped
- Salt and black pepper, to taste
- Fresh parsley, chopped, for garnish

Preparation instructions:
1. Preheat your Air Fryer to 200°C for 5 minutes.
2. In a bowl, toss diced potatoes, halloumi cubes, red and yellow bell peppers, and red onion with olive oil, salt, and black pepper.
3. Divide the mixture evenly between the two Air Fryer baskets.
4. Air fry at 200°C for 20 minutes or until the potatoes are golden and crispy, stirring halfway through the cooking time.
5. Garnish with fresh parsley before serving.

English Muffin Breakfast Pizzas

Serves: 4 / Prep time: 10 minutes / Cook time: 8 minutes

Ingredients:
- 4 whole grain English muffins, halved
- 200g tomato sauce
- 150g shredded mozzarella cheese
- 100g sliced mushrooms
- 50g sliced black olives
- 1 tsp dried oregano
- Salt and black pepper, to taste
- Fresh basil leaves, for garnish

Preparation instructions:
1. Preheat your Air Fryer to 180°C for 5 minutes.
2. Spread a layer of tomato sauce on each English muffin half.
3. Sprinkle shredded mozzarella cheese over the sauce.
4. Top with sliced mushrooms and black olives. Sprinkle with dried oregano, salt, and black

pepper.
5. Place the prepared muffins in the Air Fryer baskets.
6. Air fry at 180°C for 8 minutes or until the cheese is melted and bubbly.
7. Garnish with fresh basil leaves before serving.

Air-Fried Sausage and Hash Brown Casserole

Serves: 4 / Prep time: 15 minutes / Cook time: 25 minutes

Ingredients:
- 400g shredded hash brown potatoes
- 8 cooked sausages, sliced
- 200ml heavy cream
- 150g shredded cheddar cheese
- 1/4 tsp garlic powder • 1/4 tsp onion powder
- Salt and black pepper, to taste
- Fresh chives, chopped, for garnish

Preparation instructions:
1. Preheat your Air Fryer to 190°C for 5 minutes.
2. In a bowl, mix shredded hash brown potatoes, sliced sausages, heavy cream, shredded cheddar cheese, garlic powder, onion powder, salt, and black pepper.
3. Transfer the mixture into a baking dish suitable for the Air Fryer.
4. Place the baking dish in the Air Fryer basket.
5. Air fry at 190°C for 25 minutes or until the top is golden brown and the casserole is cooked through.
6. Garnish with fresh chives before serving.

Healthy Banana Walnut Muffins

Prep time: 15 minutes / Cook time: 20 minutes

Ingredients:
- 300g ripe bananas, mashed
- 200g whole wheat flour
- 100ml honey or maple syrup
- 60ml vegetable oil • 2 large eggs
- 1 tsp baking powder • 1/2 tsp baking soda
- 1/4 tsp salt • 1/2 tsp ground cinnamon
- 100g chopped walnuts

Preparation instructions:
1. Preheat your Air Fryer to 180°C for 5 minutes.
2. In a bowl, combine mashed bananas, whole wheat flour, honey or maple syrup, vegetable oil, eggs, baking powder, baking soda, salt, and ground cinnamon. Mix until just combined.
3. Fold in chopped walnuts.
4. Line a muffin tin with paper liners.
5. Spoon the batter evenly into the muffin cups, filling each about two-thirds full.
6. Place the muffin tin in the Air Fryer basket.
7. Air fry at 180°C for 20 minutes or until a toothpick inserted into the centre of a muffin comes out clean.
8. Allow the muffins to cool before serving.

Spinach and Feta Breakfast Pastries

Makes: 8 pastries / Prep time: 15 minutes / Cook time: 15 minutes

Ingredients:
- 1 sheet of puff pastry, thawed
- 150g fresh spinach, chopped
- 100g feta cheese, crumbled
- 1 large egg, beaten • 1/4 tsp garlic powder
- Salt and black pepper, to taste

Preparation instructions:
1. Preheat your Air Fryer to 180°C for 5 minutes.
2. In a bowl, mix chopped fresh spinach, crumbled feta cheese, beaten egg, garlic powder, salt, and black pepper.
3. Cut the puff pastry sheet into 8 equal squares.
4. Place a spoonful of the spinach and feta mixture in the centre of each pastry square.
5. Fold the pastry over the filling to create triangles. Seal the edges with a fork.
6. Place the pastries in the Air Fryer basket.
7. Air fry at 180°C for 15 minutes or until the pastries are golden brown and puffed.
8. Let the pastries cool for a few minutes before serving.

Baked Breakfast Energy Bites

Serves: 4 / Prep time: 10 minutes / Cook time: 12 minutes

Ingredients:
- 100g rolled oats • 50g almond butter
- 30ml honey • 1/2 tsp vanilla extract

- 30g dried cranberries, chopped
- 30g chopped nuts (such as almonds, walnuts, or pecans)
- 1/2 tsp ground cinnamon
- 30g dark chocolate chips

Preparation instructions:
1. Preheat your Air Fryer to 180°C (356°F) for 5 minutes.
2. In a mixing bowl, combine rolled oats, almond butter, honey, chopped dried cranberries, chopped nuts, ground cinnamon, and vanilla extract. Mix well until the ingredients are thoroughly combined.
3. Gently fold in the dark chocolate chips into the mixture.
4. Using your hands, shape the mixture into small bite-sized balls.
5. Place the energy bites in the Air Fryer basket, leaving some space between them for air circulation.
6. Bake at 180°C (356°F) for 12 minutes or until the energy bites are golden brown and firm, shaking the basket gently halfway through the cooking time to ensure even baking.
7. Remove from the Air Fryer and let the energy bites cool for a few minutes before serving.
8. Enjoy these baked breakfast energy bites as a delightful and energising snack!

Air-Fried Bubble and Squeak Patties

Serves: 4 / Prep time: 15 minutes / Cook time: 15 minutes

Ingredients:
- 500g boiled potatoes, mashed
- 200g cooked Brussels sprouts, finely chopped
- 100g cooked carrots, grated
- 1 small onion, finely chopped
- 1 garlic clove, minced
- 1 tbsp vegetable oil
- Salt and black pepper, to taste
- 2 large eggs, beaten
- 50g breadcrumbs

Preparation instructions:
1. In a large bowl, mix mashed potatoes, chopped Brussels sprouts, grated carrots, chopped onion, and minced garlic.
2. Season the mixture with salt and black pepper.
3. Shape the mixture into patties.
4. Dip each patty into beaten eggs and then coat with breadcrumbs.
5. Preheat your Air Fryer to 180°C for 5 minutes.
6. Grease the Air Fryer basket with a little oil.
7. Place the patties in the basket in a single layer, ensuring they are not touching.
8. Air fry at 180°C for 15 minutes or until the patties are golden brown and crispy.
9. Serve hot with your favourite dipping sauce.

Cheesy Bacon and Tomato Breakfast Quesadillas

Serves: 2 / Prep time: 10 minutes / Cook time: 10 minutes

Ingredients:
- 2 large flour tortillas
- 150g shredded cheddar cheese
- 4 slices of cooked bacon, chopped
- 1 large tomato, thinly sliced
- 1/2 red onion, thinly sliced
- 1 tbsp vegetable oil
- Fresh coriander, chopped, for garnish
- Sour cream, for serving

Preparation instructions:
1. Place one tortilla on a clean surface.
2. Sprinkle half of the shredded cheddar cheese on one half of the tortilla.
3. Top with half of the chopped bacon, sliced tomatoes, and red onion.
4. Sprinkle the remaining cheese over the top and fold the tortilla in half to cover the filling.
5. Repeat with the second tortilla.
6. Preheat your Air Fryer to 180°C for 5 minutes.
7. Brush both sides of the quesadillas with vegetable oil.
8. Place the quesadillas in the Air Fryer basket.
9. Air fry at 180°C for 10 minutes or until the quesadillas are golden brown and crispy.
10. Remove from the Air Fryer and let cool for a minute before slicing into wedges.
11. Garnish with fresh coriander and serve with sour cream.

Breakfast Burrito Bowls with Black Beans and Avocado

Serves: 2 / Prep time: 15 minutes / Cook time: 10 minutes

Ingredients:
- 200g cooked quinoa or rice
- 200g canned black beans, drained and rinsed
- 1 avocado, sliced
- 4 large eggs
- 1/2 tsp ground cumin
- Salt and black pepper, to taste
- 2 tbsp fresh salsa
- Fresh coriander leaves, for garnish
- Lime wedges, for serving

Preparation instructions:
1. Divide cooked quinoa or rice evenly between two bowls.
2. Top with black beans and sliced avocado.
3. Preheat your Air Fryer to 180°C for 5 minutes.
4. In a small bowl, whisk together eggs, ground cumin, salt, and black pepper.
5. Pour the egg mixture into the Air Fryer basket.
6. Air fry at 180°C, stirring occasionally, until the eggs are scrambled and cooked through, about 5-7 minutes.
7. Divide the scrambled eggs between the bowls.
8. Top each bowl with fresh salsa and garnish with fresh coriander leaves.
9. Serve with lime wedges on the side.

Air-Fried Scotch Eggs with Mustard Sauce

Serves: 4 / Prep time: 15 minutes / Cook time: 18 minutes

Ingredients:
- 4 large eggs
- 500g sausage meat
- 1/2 tsp ground sage
- 1/4 tsp black pepper
- 100g breadcrumbs
- 2 tbsp vegetable oil
- 4 tbsp Dijon mustard
- Fresh parsley, chopped, for garnish

Preparation instructions:
1. Preheat your Air Fryer to 180°C for 5 minutes.
2. Bring a pot of water to a boil and carefully add the eggs. Boil for 7 minutes, then transfer the eggs to a bowl of ice water to cool completely.
3. In a bowl, combine sausage meat, ground sage, and black pepper.
4. Peel the boiled eggs and encase each egg with the sausage mixture.
5. Roll the sausage-covered eggs in breadcrumbs to coat evenly.
6. Preheat your Air Fryer to 180°C for 5 minutes.
7. Brush each scotch egg with vegetable oil.
8. Place the scotch eggs in the Air Fryer basket.
9. Air fry at 180°C for 18 minutes or until the scotch eggs are golden brown and cooked through.
10. Mix Dijon mustard with a splash of water to create a dipping sauce.
11. Garnish the scotch eggs with chopped fresh parsley.
12. Serve hot with the mustard dipping sauce.

Cinnamon Swirl French Toast Sticks

Serves: 4 / Prep time: 15 minutes / Cook time: 10 minutes

Ingredients:
- 8 slices of wholemeal bread, cut into sticks
- 2 large eggs
- 120ml whole milk
- 1 tsp ground cinnamon
- 1/4 tsp vanilla extract
- 50g granulated sugar
- Butter, for serving
- Maple syrup, for serving

Preparation instructions:
1. Preheat your Air Fryer to 180°C for 5 minutes.
2. In a shallow dish, whisk together eggs, whole milk, ground cinnamon, and vanilla extract.
3. In another dish, spread out the granulated sugar.
4. Dip each breadstick into the egg mixture, allowing excess to drip off, then coat in sugar.
5. Place the coated sticks in a single layer in the Air Fryer baskets.
6. Air fry at 180°C for 10 minutes, turning halfway through, until golden and crispy.
7. Serve hot with butter and maple syrup.

Breakfast Stuffed Peppers with Eggs and Spinach

Serves: 4 / Prep time: 20 minutes / Cook time: 20 minutes

Ingredients:
- 4 large peppers, halved and seeds removed
- 200g fresh spinach, chopped
- 4 large eggs
- 100g feta cheese, crumbled
- Salt and black pepper, to taste
- Fresh parsley, chopped, for garnish

Preparation instructions:
1. Preheat your Air Fryer to 180°C for 5 minutes.
2. In a pan, sauté chopped spinach until wilted. Season with salt and black pepper.
3. Fill each pepper half with sautéed spinach.
4. Crack an egg into each pepper half.
5. Sprinkle crumbled feta cheese over the eggs.
6. Place the stuffed peppers in the Air Fryer baskets.
7. Air fry at 180°C for 20 minutes or until the eggs are cooked to your liking.
8. Garnish with fresh parsley before serving.

Chocolate Chip Courgette Muffins

Makes: 12 muffins / Prep time: 15 minutes / Cook time: 20 minutes

Ingredients:
- 200g grated courgette
- 2 large eggs
- 120ml vegetable oil
- 1 tsp vanilla extract
- 200g all-purpose flour
- 100g granulated sugar
- 1 tsp baking powder
- 1/2 tsp baking soda
- 1/2 tsp ground cinnamon
- 100g chocolate chips

Preparation instructions:
1. Preheat your Air Fryer to 180°C for 5 minutes.
2. In a bowl, whisk together grated courgette, eggs, vegetable oil, and vanilla extract.
3. In another bowl, combine all-purpose flour, granulated sugar, baking powder, baking soda, and ground cinnamon.
4. Gradually add the wet ingredients to the dry ingredients, stirring until just combined.
5. Fold in chocolate chips.
6. Line a muffin tin with paper liners.
7. Spoon the batter evenly into the muffin cups, filling each about two-thirds full.
8. Place the muffin tin in the Air Fryer baskets.
9. Air fry at 180°C for 20 minutes or until a toothpick inserted into the centre of a muffin comes out clean.
10. Allow the muffins to cool before serving.

Vegan Breakfast Tacos with Tofu Scramble

Serves: 4 / Prep time: 15 minutes / Cook time: 10 minutes

Ingredients:
- 300g firm tofu, crumbled
- 1 tbsp nutritional yeast
- 1/2 tsp ground turmeric
- Salt and black pepper, to taste
- 8 small corn tortillas
- 1 avocado, sliced
- Fresh salsa, for topping
- Fresh coriander, chopped, for garnish

Preparation instructions:
1. In a pan, sauté crumbled tofu with nutritional yeast, ground turmeric, salt, and black pepper until heated through and slightly crispy.
2. Warm corn tortillas in the Air Fryer at 180°C for 2 minutes.
3. Divide the tofu scramble among the warm tortillas.
4. Top with sliced avocado and fresh salsa.
5. Garnish with fresh coriander before serving.

Air-Fried Crumpets with Butter and Jam

Serves: 4 / Prep time: 5 minutes / Cook time: 5 minutes

Ingredients:
- 4 crumpets
- Butter, for spreading
- Jam or preserves, for topping
- Icing sugar, for dusting (optional)

Preparation instructions:
1. Preheat your Air Fryer to 180°C for 5 minutes.
2. Place the crumpets in the Air Fryer baskets.
3. Air fry at 180°C for 5 minutes or until the crumpets are heated through and slightly crispy on the edges.
4. Remove from the Air Fryer and spread butter over each crumpet while they are still warm.
5. Top with jam or preserves.
6. Dust with icing sugar if desired.
7. Serve hot and enjoy!

Chapter 2: Snack Recipes

Crispy Garlic Parmesan Potato Wedges

Serves: 4 / Prep time: 15 minutes / Cook time: 20 minutes

Ingredients:
- 800g potatoes, cut into wedges
- 2 tbsp olive oil
- 2 cloves garlic, minced
- 50g grated Parmesan cheese
- 1/2 tsp dried parsley
- Salt and black pepper, to taste

Preparation instructions:
1. Preheat your Air Fryer to 200°C for 5 minutes.
2. In a bowl, toss potato wedges with olive oil, minced garlic, Parmesan cheese, dried parsley, salt, and black pepper until well coated.
3. Divide the seasoned potato wedges between the two Air Fryer baskets.
4. Air fry at 200°C for 20 minutes, shaking the baskets halfway through, until the wedges are golden and crispy.
5. Serve hot, and enjoy!

Air-Fried Mini Corn Dogs with Mustard Dip

Makes: 16 mini corn dogs / Prep time: 10 minutes / Cook time: 12 minutes

Ingredients:
- 8 pork or veggie sausages, halved
- 100g cornmeal
- 50g all-purpose flour
- 1/2 tsp baking powder
- 1/4 tsp salt
- 1/4 tsp black pepper
- 120ml milk
- 1 egg
- 1 tbsp vegetable oil
- 4 tbsp mustard, for dipping

Preparation instructions:
1. Preheat your Air Fryer to 190°C for 5 minutes.
2. Insert wooden skewers into each sausage half.
3. In a bowl, whisk together cornmeal, flour, baking powder, salt, and black pepper.
4. In another bowl, mix milk, egg, and vegetable oil.
5. Dip each sausage skewer into the wet batter, then roll in the dry mixture, pressing lightly to adhere.
6. Place the coated mini corn dogs in the Air Fryer baskets.
7. Air fry at 190°C for 12 minutes or until golden brown and crispy.
8. Serve hot with mustard for dipping.

Sweet and Spicy Air-Fried Chickpeas

Serves: 4 / Prep time: 5 minutes / Cook time: 15 minutes

Ingredients:
- 400g canned chickpeas, drained and rinsed
- 1 tbsp olive oil
- 1 tbsp honey
- 1/2 tsp paprika
- 1/4 tsp cayenne pepper
- Salt, to taste

Preparation instructions:
1. Preheat your Air Fryer to 180°C for 5 minutes.
2. In a bowl, toss chickpeas with olive oil, honey, paprika, cayenne pepper, and salt until well coated.
3. Spread the chickpeas in a single layer in the Air Fryer baskets.
4. Air fry at 180°C for 15 minutes, shaking the baskets occasionally, until the chickpeas are crispy and golden.
5. Remove from the Air Fryer and let cool for a few minutes before serving.

Cheese and Bacon Stuffed Mushrooms

Serves: 4 / Prep time: 10 minutes / Cook time: 15 minutes

Ingredients:
- 8 large mushrooms, stems removed and

reserved
- 50g cream cheese
- 50g grated cheddar cheese
- 4 slices bacon, cooked and crumbled
- 2 cloves garlic, minced
- Salt and black pepper, to taste
- Fresh parsley, chopped, for garnish

Preparation instructions:
1. Preheat your Air Fryer to 180°C for 5 minutes.
2. Finely chop the reserved mushroom stems.
3. In a bowl, mix cream cheese, cheddar cheese, chopped mushroom stems, crumbled bacon, minced garlic, salt, and black pepper until well combined.
4. Stuff each mushroom cap with the cheese and bacon mixture.
5. Place the stuffed mushrooms in the Air Fryer baskets.
6. Air fry at 180°C for 15 minutes or until the mushrooms are tender and the filling is golden and bubbly.
7. Garnish with chopped fresh parsley before serving.

Crunchy Air-Fried Pickles with Ranch Dip

Serves: 4 / Prep time: 10 minutes / Cook time: 10 minutes

Ingredients:
- 200g dill pickle slices, drained
- 50g all-purpose flour
- 1/2 tsp garlic powder
- 1/2 tsp paprika
- 1/4 tsp cayenne pepper
- Salt and black pepper, to taste
- 1 large egg, beaten
- 50g breadcrumbs
- Cooking spray
- 120ml ranch dressing, for dipping

Preparation instructions:
1. Preheat your Air Fryer to 200°C for 5 minutes.
2. In a bowl, combine flour, garlic powder, paprika, cayenne pepper, salt, and black pepper.
3. Dip pickle slices into the flour mixture, then into the beaten egg, and finally into the breadcrumbs, pressing lightly to adhere.
4. Place the coated pickles in a single layer in the Air Fryer baskets.
5. Lightly spray the pickles with cooking spray.
6. Air fry at 200°C for 10 minutes or until the pickles are golden and crispy.
7. Serve hot with ranch dressing for dipping. Enjoy your crunchy pickles!

Air-Fried Mozzarella Sticks with Marinara Sauce

Serves: 4 / Prep time: 15 minutes / Cook time: 10 minutes

Ingredients:
- 200g mozzarella cheese, cut into sticks
- 50g all-purpose flour
- 2 large eggs, beaten
- 100g breadcrumbs
- 1/2 tsp dried oregano
- 1/2 tsp garlic powder
- 1/4 tsp black pepper
- Cooking spray
- 200ml marinara sauce, for dipping

Preparation instructions:
1. Preheat your Air Fryer to 200°C for 5 minutes.
2. Coat mozzarella sticks in flour, dip in beaten eggs, and roll in a mixture of breadcrumbs, dried oregano, garlic powder, and black pepper, pressing gently to adhere.
3. Place the coated mozzarella sticks in a single layer in the Air Fryer baskets.
4. Lightly spray the sticks with cooking spray.
5. Air fry at 200°C for 10 minutes or until the mozzarella sticks are golden and crispy.
6. Serve hot with marinara sauce for dipping.

Sticky Honey Mustard Chicken Wings

Serves: 4 / Prep time: 15 minutes / Cook time: 25 minutes

Ingredients:
- 800g chicken wings
- 2 tbsp honey

- 2 tbsp Dijon mustard
- 1 tbsp soy sauce
- 1/2 tsp garlic powder
- 1/2 tsp paprika
- Salt and black pepper, to taste
- Fresh chives, chopped, for garnish

Preparation instructions:
1. Preheat your Air Fryer to 200°C for 5 minutes.
2. In a bowl, whisk together honey, Dijon mustard, soy sauce, garlic powder, paprika, salt, and black pepper.
3. Toss chicken wings in the honey mustard mixture until well coated.
4. Place the coated chicken wings in the Air Fryer baskets.
5. Air fry at 200°C for 25 minutes, shaking the baskets occasionally, until the wings are cooked through and sticky.
6. Garnish with chopped fresh chives before serving.

Spinach and Artichoke Stuffed Wontons

Makes: 16 wontons / Prep time: 20 minutes / Cook time: 8 minutes

Ingredients:
- 100g frozen spinach, thawed and drained
- 150g canned artichoke hearts, chopped
- 50g cream cheese, softened
- 1/4 tsp garlic powder
- 1/4 tsp onion powder
- 16 wonton wrappers
- Cooking spray
- Sweet chilli sauce, for dipping

Preparation instructions:
1. Preheat your Air Fryer to 180°C for 5 minutes.
2. In a bowl, mix together thawed spinach, chopped artichoke hearts, cream cheese, garlic powder, and onion powder until well combined.
3. Place a spoonful of the spinach and artichoke mixture in the centre of each wonton wrapper.
4. Moisten the edges of the wrapper with water and fold it diagonally to create a triangle, pressing to seal the edges.
5. Lightly spray the stuffed wontons with cooking spray.
6. Place the stuffed wontons in a single layer in the Air Fryer baskets.
7. Air fry at 180°C for 8 minutes or until the wontons are golden and crispy.
8. Serve hot with sweet chilli sauce for dipping.

Air-Fried Vegetable Spring Rolls

Makes: 8 spring rolls / Prep time: 20 minutes / Cook time: 10 minutes

Ingredients:
- 100g vermicelli noodles, soaked in hot water and drained
- 1 carrot, julienned
- 1 bell pepper, thinly sliced
- 50g bean sprouts
- 8 spring roll wrappers
- 1 tbsp soy sauce
- 1 tbsp hoisin sauce
- 1/2 tsp garlic powder
- 1/2 tsp ground ginger
- Cooking spray
- Sweet and sour sauce, for dipping

Preparation instructions:
1. Preheat your Air Fryer to 200°C for 5 minutes.
2. In a bowl, combine vermicelli noodles, julienned carrot, sliced bell pepper, bean sprouts, soy sauce, hoisin sauce, garlic powder, and ground ginger.
3. Place a spoonful of the vegetable mixture on one end of a spring roll wrapper. Roll tightly, folding in the sides, and seal the edge with water.
4. Lightly spray the vegetable spring rolls with cooking spray.
5. Place the spring rolls in a single layer in the Air Fryer baskets.
6. Air fry at 200°C for 10 minutes or until the spring rolls are golden and crispy.
7. Serve hot with sweet and sour sauce for dipping.

Crispy Coconut Shrimp with Mango Dipping Sauce

Serves: 4 / Prep time: 15 minutes / Cook time: 10 minutes

Ingredients:
- 200g large shrimp, peeled and deveined

- 50g all-purpose flour
- 2 large eggs, beaten
- 100g desiccated coconut
- Cooking spray
- 1 ripe mango, peeled and diced
- 1/4 tsp chilli flakes
- 1 tbsp fresh lime juice
- Fresh coriander, chopped, for garnish

Preparation instructions:
1. Preheat your Air Fryer to 200°C for 5 minutes.
2. Dredge each shrimp in flour, dip in beaten eggs, and roll in desiccated coconut, pressing gently to adhere.
3. Place the coated shrimp in a single layer in the Air Fryer baskets.
4. Lightly spray the shrimp with cooking spray.
5. Air fry at 200°C for 10 minutes or until the shrimp are golden and crispy.
6. In a blender, combine diced mango, chilli flakes, and lime juice. Blend until smooth to make the dipping sauce.
7. Garnish the crispy coconut shrimp with chopped fresh coriander.
8. Serve hot with mango dipping sauce. Enjoy your crunchy coconut shrimp!

Spiced Sweet Potato Fries with Chipotle Aioli

Serves: 4 / Prep time: 15 minutes / Cook time: 20 minutes

Ingredients:
- 600g sweet potatoes, cut into fries
- 2 tbsp olive oil
- 1 tsp paprika
- 1/2 tsp ground cumin
- 1/4 tsp cayenne pepper
- Salt and black pepper, to taste
- Cooking spray
- 120ml mayonnaise
- 1 tbsp chipotle peppers in adobo sauce, minced

Preparation instructions:
1. Preheat your Air Fryer to 200°C for 5 minutes.
2. In a bowl, toss sweet potato fries with olive oil, paprika, ground cumin, cayenne pepper, salt, and black pepper until well coated.
3. Divide the seasoned sweet potato fries between the two Air Fryer baskets.
4. Lightly spray the fries with cooking spray.
5. Air fry at 200°C for 20 minutes, shaking the baskets halfway through, until the fries are crispy and golden.
6. In a small bowl, mix together mayonnaise and minced chipotle peppers to prepare the aioli.
7. Serve the spiced sweet potato fries hot with chipotle aioli for dipping.

Buffalo Cauliflower Bites with Blue Cheese Dip

Serves: 4 / Prep time: 15 minutes / Cook time: 20 minutes

Ingredients:
- 1 medium cauliflower, cut into florets
- 50g all-purpose flour
- 1/2 tsp garlic powder
- 1/2 tsp onion powder
- 1/2 tsp paprika
- 1/4 tsp cayenne pepper
- Salt and black pepper, to taste
- 120ml buffalo sauce
- 120ml sour cream
- 50g blue cheese, crumbled

Preparation instructions:
1. Preheat your Air Fryer to 200°C for 5 minutes.
2. In a bowl, combine cauliflower florets, all-purpose flour, garlic powder, onion powder, paprika, cayenne pepper, salt, and black pepper, tossing until well coated.
3. Divide the seasoned cauliflower between the two Air Fryer baskets.
4. Air fry at 200°C for 20 minutes, shaking the baskets occasionally, until the cauliflower is crispy and golden.
5. In a small saucepan, heat buffalo sauce over low heat.
6. Toss the cooked cauliflower in the heated buffalo sauce to coat evenly.

7. In another bowl, mix sour cream and crumbled blue cheese to prepare the dip.
8. Serve the buffalo cauliflower bites hot with blue cheese dip on the side.

Air-Fried Jalapeño Poppers with Cream Cheese Filling

Serves: 4 / Prep time: 20 minutes / Cook time: 15 minutes

Ingredients:
- 8 large jalapeño peppers, halved and seeds removed
- 150g cream cheese, softened
- 50g grated cheddar cheese
- 1/4 tsp garlic powder
- Salt and black pepper, to taste
- 50g all-purpose flour
- 2 large eggs, beaten
- 100g breadcrumbs
- Cooking spray

Preparation instructions:
1. Preheat your Air Fryer to 200°C for 5 minutes.
2. In a bowl, mix together softened cream cheese, grated cheddar cheese, garlic powder, salt, and black pepper until well combined.
3. Spoon the cream cheese filling into each jalapeño half.
4. Dredge each stuffed jalapeño in all-purpose flour, dip in beaten eggs, and roll in breadcrumbs, pressing gently to adhere.
5. Place the coated jalapeño poppers in a single layer in the Air Fryer baskets.
6. Lightly spray the poppers with cooking spray.
7. Air fry at 200°C for 15 minutes or until the poppers are golden and crispy.
8. Serve hot. Be cautious, they might be hot inside!

Mediterranean Stuffed Peppers

Serves: 4 / Prep time: 20 minutes / Cook time: 25 minutes

Ingredients:
- 4 large peppers, halved and seeds removed
- 200g cooked quinoa
- 100g crumbled feta cheese
- 50g black olives, sliced
- 1/4 tsp dried oregano
- 1/4 tsp dried basil
- Salt and black pepper, to taste
- 2 tbsp olive oil

Preparation instructions:
1. Preheat your Air Fryer to 180°C for 5 minutes.
2. In a bowl, combine cooked quinoa, crumbled feta cheese, sliced black olives, dried oregano, dried basil, salt, and black pepper.
3. Fill each pepper half with the quinoa mixture.
4. Drizzle olive oil over the stuffed peppers.
5. Place the stuffed peppers in the Air Fryer baskets.
6. Air fry at 180°C for 25 minutes or until the peppers are tender.
7. Serve hot and enjoy the Mediterranean flavours!

Caprese Skewers with Balsamic Glaze

Serves: 4 / Prep time: 15 minutes / Cook time: 5 minutes

Ingredients:
- 16 cherry tomatoes
- 16 fresh mozzarella balls
- 16 fresh basil leaves
- 2 tbsp olive oil
- Salt and black pepper, to taste
- 60ml balsamic glaze

Preparation instructions:
1. Preheat your Air Fryer to 180°C for 5 minutes.
2. On small skewers, thread a cherry tomato, a fresh mozzarella ball, and a basil leaf, repeating once more for each skewer.
3. Brush the skewers with olive oil and season with salt and black pepper.
4. Place the caprese skewers in the Air Fryer baskets.
5. Air fry at 180°C for 5 minutes or until the cheese starts to melt and the tomatoes are slightly softened.
6. Drizzle the caprese skewers with balsamic

glaze before serving.
7. Serve hot and savour the delightful Mediterranean taste!

Panko-Crusted Fish Tacos with Lime Crema

Serves: 4 / Prep time: 15 minutes / Cook time: 12 minutes

Ingredients:
- 400g white fish fillets, cut into strips
- 100g panko breadcrumbs
- 1/2 tsp paprika
- 1/2 tsp garlic powder
- 1/4 tsp cayenne pepper
- Salt and black pepper, to taste
- Cooking spray
- 8 small corn tortillas
- 1 avocado, sliced
- Fresh coriander, chopped, for garnish
- Lime wedges, for serving
- Lime Crema:
- 120ml sour cream
- Zest and juice of 1 lime
- Salt and black pepper, to taste

Preparation instructions:
1. Preheat your Air Fryer to 200°C for 5 minutes.
2. In a bowl, combine panko breadcrumbs, paprika, garlic powder, cayenne pepper, salt, and black pepper.
3. Dredge fish strips in the breadcrumb mixture, pressing gently to adhere.
4. Lightly spray the breaded fish with cooking spray.
5. Place the fish in a single layer in the Air Fryer baskets.
6. Air fry at 200°C for 12 minutes or until the fish is crispy and golden.
7. While the fish cooks, prepare the lime crema by mixing sour cream with lime zest, lime juice, salt, and black pepper.
8. Warm the corn tortillas in the Air Fryer for 2 minutes.
9. Assemble tacos with crispy fish strips, sliced avocado, a drizzle of lime crema, and a sprinkle of fresh coriander.
10. Serve hot with lime wedges on the side.

Mini Beef and Mushroom Wellingtons

Makes: 4 Wellingtons / Prep time: 20 minutes / Cook time: 18 minutes

Ingredients:
- 400g beef fillet steaks
- 200g mushrooms, finely chopped
- 1 small onion, finely chopped
- 2 tbsp fresh parsley, chopped
- Salt and black pepper, to taste
- 4 slices of Parma ham
- 400g puff pastry, rolled out
- 1 egg, beaten, for egg wash

Preparation instructions:
1. Preheat your Air Fryer to 200°C for 5 minutes.
2. In a pan, sauté mushrooms and onions until soft. Stir in fresh parsley, salt, and black pepper. Let the mixture cool.
3. Season beef fillet steaks with salt and black pepper.
4. Wrap each fillet with a slice of Parma ham.
5. Divide the mushroom mixture into 4 portions and place it on top of each Parma ham-wrapped fillet.
6. Roll out puff pastry and cut into 4 squares.
7. Place each fillet in the centre of a pastry square. Fold the pastry around the fillet, sealing the edges.
8. Brush the pastry with beaten egg for a golden finish.
9. Place the Wellingtons in the Air Fryer baskets.
10. Air fry at 200°C for 18 minutes or until the pastry is puffed and golden.
11. Let them rest for a few minutes before serving. Enjoy your mini Beef and Mushroom Wellingtons!

Air-Fried Falafel with Tahini Sauce

Makes: 16 falafel balls / Prep time: 15 minutes / Cook time: 15 minutes

Ingredients:
- 400g canned chickpeas, drained and rinsed
- 1 small onion, chopped
- 2 cloves garlic, minced
- 2 tbsp fresh parsley, chopped
- 1 tsp ground cumin
- 1/2 tsp ground coriander
- 1/4 tsp cayenne pepper
- Salt and black pepper, to taste
- 2 tbsp chickpea flour
- Cooking spray
- Tahini Sauce:
- 120ml tahini paste
- 2 tbsp lemon juice
- 2 tbsp water
- Salt, to taste

Preparation instructions:
1. Preheat your Air Fryer to 200°C for 5 minutes.
2. In a food processor, blend chickpeas, chopped onion, minced garlic, fresh parsley, ground cumin, ground coriander, cayenne pepper, salt, and black pepper until smooth.
3. Transfer the mixture to a bowl and stir in chickpea flour to bind.
4. Form the mixture into small balls and place them on a tray lined with parchment paper.
5. Lightly spray the falafel balls with cooking spray.
6. Place the falafel balls in a single layer in the Air Fryer baskets.
7. Air fry at 200°C for 15 minutes or until the falafel is crispy and golden.
8. While the falafel cooks, prepare the tahini sauce by mixing tahini paste, lemon juice, water, and salt until smooth.
9. Serve the hot falafel with tahini sauce for dipping.

Crispy Polenta Fries with Marinara Dip

Serves: 4 / Prep time: 15 minutes / Cook time: 20 minutes

Ingredients:
- 400g polenta, cooled and cut into fries
- 50g grated Parmesan cheese
- 1/2 tsp dried thyme
- 1/2 tsp smoked paprika
- Salt and black pepper, to taste
- Cooking spray
- 240ml marinara sauce, for dipping

Preparation instructions:
1. Preheat your Air Fryer to 200°C for 5 minutes.
2. In a bowl, combine polenta fries, grated Parmesan cheese, dried thyme, smoked paprika, salt, and black pepper, tossing until well coated.
3. Divide the seasoned polenta fries between the two Air Fryer baskets.
4. Lightly spray the fries with cooking spray.
5. Air fry at 200°C for 20 minutes, shaking the baskets halfway through, until the fries are crispy and golden.
6. Serve the crispy polenta fries hot with marinara sauce for dipping.

Raspberry and Nutella Wonton Purses

Makes: 16 wonton purses / Prep time: 15 minutes / Cook time: 8 minutes

Ingredients:
- 16 wonton wrappers
- 8 tsp raspberry jam
- Icing sugar, for dusting
- 8 tsp Nutella
- Cooking spray

Preparation instructions:
1. Preheat your Air Fryer to 180°C for 5 minutes.
2. Place a teaspoon of Nutella and a teaspoon of raspberry jam in the centre of each wonton wrapper.
3. Fold the wrappers into a purse shape, pinching the edges to seal.
4. Lightly spray the wonton purses with cooking spray.
5. Place the wonton purses in a single layer in the Air Fryer baskets.
6. Air fry at 180°C for 8 minutes or until the purses are golden and crispy.
7. Let them cool for a few minutes before dusting with icing sugar.
8. Serve warm and enjoy the delightful Raspberry and Nutella Wonton Purses!

Chapter 3: Lunch Recipes

Crispy Chicken Sandwich with Coleslaw

Serves: 4 / Prep time: 15 minutes / Cook time: 15 minutes

Ingredients:
- 4 boneless, skinless chicken breasts
- 100g plain flour
- 2 eggs, beaten
- 100g breadcrumbs
- 1/2 tsp paprika
- 1/2 tsp garlic powder
- Salt and black pepper, to taste
- Cooking spray
- 4 burger buns
- 100g coleslaw

Preparation instructions:
1. Preheat your Air Fryer to 200°C for 5 minutes.
2. Season chicken breasts with salt, black pepper, paprika, and garlic powder.
3. Dredge each chicken breast in flour, dip in beaten eggs, and coat with breadcrumbs.
4. Lightly spray each breaded chicken breast with cooking spray.
5. Place the chicken breasts in a single layer in the Air Fryer baskets.
6. Air fry at 200°C for 15 minutes, turning halfway through, until the chicken is golden and crispy.
7. Toast the burger buns in the Air Fryer for 2 minutes.
8. Assemble sandwiches with crispy chicken breasts and a generous layer of coleslaw.
9. Serve hot and enjoy your Crispy Chicken Sandwich!

Air-Fried Fish and Chips with Tartar Sauce

Serves: 4 / Prep time: 20 minutes / Cook time: 20 minutes

Ingredients:
- 4 white fish fillets
- 100g plain flour
- 2 eggs, beaten
- 100g breadcrumbs
- 1/2 tsp paprika
- 1/2 tsp garlic powder
- Salt and black pepper, to taste
- Cooking spray
- 800g potatoes, cut into chips
- 120ml tartar sauce

Preparation instructions:
1. Preheat your Air Fryer to 200°C for 5 minutes.
2. Season fish fillets with salt, black pepper, paprika, and garlic powder.
3. Dredge each fillet in flour, dip in beaten eggs, and coat with breadcrumbs.
4. Lightly spray each breaded fish fillet with cooking spray.
5. Place the fish fillets in a single layer in the Air Fryer baskets.
6. Air fry at 200°C for 15 minutes, turning halfway through, until the fish is crispy and golden.
7. In another basket, toss potato chips with a little cooking spray and salt.
8. Air fry the chips at 200°C for 20 minutes or until golden and crispy, shaking the basket occasionally.
9. Serve the fish and chips hot with tartar sauce on the side.

Veggie-Stuffed Air-Fried Calzone

Serves: 4 / Prep time: 15 minutes / Cook time: 15 minutes

Ingredients:
- 400g pizza dough
- 100g tomato sauce
- 1 red bell pepper, diced
- 1 yellow bell pepper, diced
- 1 small red onion, finely chopped
- 100g mushrooms, sliced
- 100g mozzarella cheese, shredded
- 1 tbsp olive oil
- Salt and black pepper, to taste

Preparation instructions:
1. Preheat your Air Fryer to 200°C for 5 minutes.
2. Divide the pizza dough into 4 equal portions.
3. Roll out each portion into a circle on a

lightly floured surface.
4. Spread tomato sauce on half of each dough circle, leaving a border around the edge.
5. Top the sauce with diced bell peppers, chopped red onion, and sliced mushrooms.
6. Sprinkle mozzarella cheese over the veggies.
7. Fold the dough over the filling, forming a half-moon shape, and press the edges to seal.
8. Brush the calzones with olive oil and season with salt and black pepper.
9. Place the calzones in a single layer in the Air Fryer baskets.
10. Air fry at 200°C for 15 minutes or until the calzones are golden and crispy.
11. Serve hot and enjoy your Veggie-Stuffed Calzone!

Air Fryer Pesto Chicken Pasta Salad

Serves: 4 / Prep time: 15 minutes / Cook time: 10 minutes

Ingredients:
- 300g pasta, cooked and cooled
- 2 chicken breasts, seasoned and air-fried, then shredded
- 100g cherry tomatoes, halved
- 50g black olives, sliced
- 50g feta cheese, crumbled
- 4 tbsp pesto sauce
- 2 tbsp olive oil
- Salt and black pepper, to taste
- Fresh basil leaves, for garnish

Preparation instructions:
1. Season the chicken breasts with salt, pepper, and a little olive oil.
2. Preheat the Air Fryer to 180°C (356°F) for 5 minutes.
3. Air fry the chicken breasts for 8-10 minutes or until cooked through. Let them cool, then shred the chicken.
4. Cook the pasta according to the package instructions until al dente. Drain and let it cool.
5. In a large bowl, combine the cooked pasta, shredded chicken, cherry tomatoes, black olives, and crumbled feta cheese.
6. In a small bowl, whisk together pesto sauce and olive oil until well combined.
7. Pour the pesto dressing over the pasta mixture and toss until all ingredients are evenly coated.
8. Season the salad with salt and black pepper to taste.
9. Garnish with fresh basil leaves for a burst of color and added freshness.
10. Serve the Pesto Chicken Pasta Salad chilled, and enjoy the delightful flavors and textures brought together in your Air Fryer creation!

Air-Fried Falafel Wrap with Hummus

Serves: 4 / Prep time: 15 minutes / Cook time: 15 minutes

Ingredients:
- 400g canned chickpeas, drained and rinsed
- 1 small onion, chopped
- 2 cloves garlic, minced
- 2 tbsp fresh parsley, chopped
- 1 tsp ground cumin
- 1/2 tsp ground coriander
- Salt and black pepper, to taste
- 2 tbsp chickpea flour
- Cooking spray
- 4 whole wheat wraps
- 200g hummus
- Fresh lettuce leaves, for wrapping

Preparation instructions:
1. Preheat your Air Fryer to 200°C for 5 minutes.
2. In a food processor, blend chickpeas, chopped onion, minced garlic, fresh parsley, ground cumin, ground coriander, salt, and black pepper until smooth.
3. Transfer the mixture to a bowl and stir in chickpea flour to bind.
4. Form the mixture into small falafel balls.
5. Lightly spray the falafel balls with cooking spray.
6. Place the falafel balls in a single layer in the Air Fryer baskets.
7. Air fry at 200°C for 15 minutes or until the falafel is crispy and golden.
8. Warm the whole wheat wraps in the Air Fryer for 2 minutes.

9. Spread a generous layer of hummus on each wrap.
10. Place falafel balls and fresh lettuce leaves on top of the hummus.
11. Roll up the wraps, folding in the sides, to secure the filling.
12. Serve your Air-Fried Falafel Wraps with Hummus and enjoy this delightful dish!

BBQ Pulled Pork Sliders

Serves: 4 / Prep time: 15 minutes / Cook time: 8 hours (slow cooker time) / Air fry time: 10 minutes

Ingredients:
- 400g pork shoulder, trimmed and cubed
- 240ml BBQ sauce
- 4 small burger buns
- 100g coleslaw
- Fresh parsley, for garnish

Preparation instructions:
1. Place pork shoulder cubes and BBQ sauce in a slow cooker. Cook on low for 8 hours until pork is tender and easily shredded.
2. Shred the cooked pork using two forks.
3. Preheat the Air Fryer to 200°C for 5 minutes.
4. Split the burger buns and lightly toast in the Air Fryer for 2 minutes.
5. Fill the buns with BBQ pulled pork and top with coleslaw.
6. Garnish with fresh parsley and serve hot.

Crispy Halloumi and Vegetable Skewers

Serves: 4 / Prep time: 20 minutes / Cook time: 10 minutes

Ingredients:
- 250g halloumi cheese, cut into cubes
- 1 red bell pepper, cut into chunks
- 1 yellow bell pepper, cut into chunks
- 1 red onion, cut into chunks
- 8 cherry tomatoes
- 2 tbsp olive oil
- 1 tsp smoked paprika
- Salt and black pepper, to taste
- Fresh lemon wedges, for serving

Preparation instructions:
1. In a bowl, combine halloumi cubes, bell peppers, red onion, and cherry tomatoes.
2. Drizzle with olive oil, sprinkle with smoked paprika, salt, and black pepper. Toss to coat evenly.
3. Thread the marinated vegetables and halloumi onto skewers.
4. Preheat the Air Fryer to 200°C for 5 minutes.
5. Place the skewers in the Air Fryer baskets. Air fry for 10 minutes or until the halloumi is crispy and vegetables are tender.
6. Serve hot with fresh lemon wedges.

Mushroom and Spinach Stuffed Chicken Breast

Serves: 4 / Prep time: 20 minutes / Cook time: 25 minutes

Ingredients:
- 4 chicken breasts
- 200g mushrooms, finely chopped
- 100g fresh spinach, chopped
- 1 garlic clove, minced
- 50g feta cheese, crumbled
- 1 tbsp olive oil
- Salt and black pepper, to taste
- Fresh parsley, for garnish

Preparation instructions:
1. Preheat the Air Fryer to 180°C for 5 minutes.
2. In a pan, heat olive oil. Add mushrooms and garlic, sauté until tender. Add spinach and cook until wilted. Remove from heat and let cool.
3. Slice a pocket into each chicken breast.
4. Stuff each chicken breast with the mushroom-spinach mixture and crumbled feta cheese. Secure with toothpicks.
5. Season chicken breasts with salt and black pepper.
6. Preheat the Air Fryer to 200°C for 5 minutes.
7. Place the stuffed chicken breasts in the Air Fryer baskets. Air fry for 25 minutes or until the chicken is cooked through.
8. Garnish with fresh parsley and serve hot.

Air-Fried Sweet Potato and Chickpea Patties

Serves: 4 / Prep time: 15 minutes / Cook time:

20 minutes

Ingredients:
- 400g sweet potatoes, peeled and grated
- 400g canned chickpeas, drained and rinsed
- 1 small red onion, finely chopped
- 1 garlic clove, minced
- 1 tsp ground cumin
- 1 tsp ground coriander
- Salt and black pepper, to taste
- 2 tbsp chickpea flour
- Cooking spray
- Yoghurt sauce, for dipping

Preparation instructions:
1. In a bowl, combine grated sweet potatoes, chickpeas, red onion, garlic, ground cumin, ground coriander, salt, black pepper, and chickpea flour. Mix until well combined.
2. Form the mixture into patties.
3. Preheat the Air Fryer to 180°C for 5 minutes.
4. Lightly spray the patties with cooking spray.
5. Place the patties in the Air Fryer baskets. Air fry for 20 minutes or until the patties are golden and crispy, turning halfway through.
6. Serve hot with yoghurt sauce for dipping.

Spicy Shrimp Tacos with coriander Lime Slaw

Serves: 4 / Prep time: 20 minutes / Cook time: 10 minutes

Ingredients:
- 400g large shrimp, peeled and deveined
- 1 tbsp olive oil
- 1 tsp chilli powder
- 1/2 tsp paprika
- 1/2 tsp cayenne pepper
- Salt and black pepper, to taste
- 8 small corn tortillas
- 200g cabbage, thinly sliced
- 60g fresh coriander, chopped
- 2 tbsp mayonnaise
- Juice of 1 lime
- 1 avocado, sliced

Preparation instructions:
1. In a bowl, combine shrimp, olive oil, chilli powder, paprika, cayenne pepper, salt, and black pepper. Toss to coat shrimp evenly.
2. Preheat the Air Fryer to 200°C for 5 minutes.
3. Place the seasoned shrimp in the Air Fryer baskets. Air fry for 8-10 minutes or until the shrimp are cooked through and slightly crispy.
4. Warm the corn tortillas in the Air Fryer for 2 minutes.
5. In a bowl, combine sliced cabbage, fresh coriander, mayonnaise, and lime juice. Toss to make the slaw.
6. Assemble tacos with spicy shrimp, coriander lime slaw, and avocado slices.
7. Serve hot and enjoy your Spicy Shrimp Tacos!

Mediterranean Quinoa Salad with Feta

Serves: 4 / Prep time: 15 minutes / Cook time: 15 minutes

Ingredients:
- 200g quinoa, rinsed and drained
- 400ml vegetable broth
- 100g cherry tomatoes, halved
- 1 cucumber, diced
- 60g Kalamata olives, pitted and halved
- 100g feta cheese, crumbled
- 2 tbsp olive oil
- Juice of 1 lemon
- 1 tsp dried oregano
- Salt and black pepper, to taste
- Fresh parsley, for garnish

Preparation instructions:
1. In a basket-style air fryer, combine quinoa and vegetable broth. Cook at 180°C (356°F) for 15 minutes or until quinoa is cooked and liquid is absorbed. Let it cool.
2. In a large bowl, combine the cooked quinoa, cherry tomatoes, diced cucumber, Kalamata olives, and crumbled feta cheese.
3. In a small bowl, whisk together olive oil, lemon juice, dried oregano, salt, and black pepper.
4. Pour the dressing over the quinoa mixture. Toss gently to combine, ensuring the salad is well coated with the dressing.
5. Garnish the salad with freshly chopped parsley for a burst of color and added

freshness.
6. Serve your Air Fryer Mediterranean Quinoa Salad chilled, enjoying the vibrant flavors of the Mediterranean in every bite.

Air-Fried Aubergine Parmesan

Serves: 4 / Prep time: 20 minutes / Cook time: 18 minutes

Ingredients:
- 1 large aubergine, sliced into 1 cm thick rounds
- 100g breadcrumbs
- 50g grated Parmesan cheese
- 2 large eggs, beaten
- 400g marinara sauce
- 200g mozzarella cheese, shredded
- Fresh basil leaves, for garnish

Preparation instructions:
1. Preheat the Air Fryer to 190°C for 5 minutes.
2. In one bowl, combine breadcrumbs and grated Parmesan cheese. Dip each aubergine slice in beaten eggs, then coat with breadcrumb mixture.
3. Place the coated aubergine slices in a single layer in the Air Fryer baskets. Air fry for 18 minutes or until crispy and golden brown.
4. In a baking dish, spread a thin layer of marinara sauce. Arrange half of the cooked aubergine slices over the sauce. Top with more marinara sauce and half of the shredded mozzarella cheese. Repeat the layers.
5. Bake in the Air Fryer for an additional 5 minutes or until the cheese is melted and bubbly.
6. Garnish with fresh basil leaves and serve your Air-Fried aubergine Parmesan hot.

Classic BLT Sandwich with Avocado

Serves: 4 / Prep time: 10 minutes / Cook time: 5 minutes

Ingredients:
- 8 slices of bread
- 200g bacon, cooked until crispy
- 2 large tomatoes, sliced
- 1 avocado, sliced
- Lettuce leaves
- 4 tbsp mayonnaise
- Salt and black pepper, to taste

Preparation instructions:
1. Preheat the Air Fryer to 180°C for 5 minutes.
2. Place bacon slices in the Air Fryer baskets and air fry for 5 minutes or until crispy. Remove and drain on paper towels.
3. Toast the bread slices in the Air Fryer for 2 minutes.
4. Spread mayonnaise on one side of each bread slice.
5. Assemble the sandwiches by layering lettuce leaves, tomato slices, crispy bacon, and avocado slices between the bread slices.
6. Season with salt and black pepper to taste.
7. Serve your Classic BLT Sandwiches with Avocado immediately.

Lemon Herb Air-Fried Salmon

Serves: 4 / Prep time: 10 minutes / Cook time: 12 minutes

Ingredients:
- 4 salmon fillets
- Zest and juice of 1 lemon
- 2 tbsp olive oil
- 1 garlic clove, minced
- 1 tsp dried basil
- 1 tsp dried parsley
- Salt and black pepper, to taste
- Fresh dill, for garnish

Preparation instructions:
1. Preheat the Air Fryer to 200°C for 5 minutes.
2. In a bowl, whisk together lemon zest, lemon juice, olive oil, minced garlic, dried basil, dried parsley, salt, and black pepper.
3. Brush the salmon fillets with the lemon herb mixture.
4. Place the salmon fillets in the Air Fryer baskets. Air fry for 12 minutes or until the salmon is cooked through and flakes easily with a fork.
5. Garnish with fresh dill and serve your Lemon Herb Air-Fried Salmon hot.

Teriyaki Tofu Stir Fry with Vegetables

Serves: 4 / Prep time: 15 minutes / Cook time: 10 minutes

Ingredients:
- 400g firm tofu, pressed and cubed
- 200g broccoli florets
- 1 red pepper, sliced
- 1 yellow pepper, sliced
- 1 carrot, julienned
- 4 tbsp teriyaki sauce
- 2 tbsp soy sauce
- 1 tbsp sesame oil
- 1 tbsp cornstarch
- 2 tbsp water
- Sesame seeds, for garnish
- Green onions, sliced, for garnish

Preparation instructions:
1. Preheat the Air Fryer to 200°C for 5 minutes.
2. In a bowl, combine cubed tofu, broccoli florets, sliced red pepper, sliced yellow pepper, and julienned carrot.
3. In a separate bowl, whisk together teriyaki sauce, soy sauce, sesame oil, cornstarch, and water to make the sauce.
4. Pour the sauce over the tofu and vegetable mixture. Toss to coat evenly.
5. Place the tofu and vegetable mixture in the Air Fryer baskets. Air fry for 10 minutes, shaking the baskets halfway through cooking.
6. Garnish with sesame seeds and sliced green onions. Serve your Teriyaki Tofu Stir Fry with Vegetables over rice or noodles.

Spinach and Feta Stuffed Portobello Mushrooms

Serves: 4 / Prep time: 15 minutes / Cook time: 12 minutes

Ingredients:
- 4 large Portobello mushrooms
- 200g fresh spinach, chopped
- 100g feta cheese, crumbled
- 2 cloves garlic, minced
- 2 tbsp olive oil
- Salt and black pepper, to taste
- Fresh parsley, chopped, for garnish

Preparation instructions:
1. Preheat the Air Fryer to 180°C for 5 minutes.
2. Remove the stems from the Portobello mushrooms and gently scrape out the gills. Brush the mushrooms with olive oil and season with salt and black pepper.
3. In a pan, heat 1 tablespoon of olive oil over medium heat. Add minced garlic and chopped spinach. Sauté until the spinach wilts. Remove from heat and stir in crumbled feta cheese.
4. Stuff the Portobello mushrooms with the spinach and feta mixture.
5. Place the stuffed mushrooms in the Air Fryer baskets. Air fry for 12 minutes or until the mushrooms are tender and the filling is heated through.
6. Garnish with fresh parsley and serve your Spinach and Feta Stuffed Portobello Mushrooms hot.

Air-Fried Prawn and Mango Salad

Serves: 4 / Prep time: 15 minutes / Cook time: 6 minutes

Ingredients:
- 300g large prawns, peeled and deveined
- 1 ripe mango, peeled and diced
- 100g mixed salad greens
- 1 cucumber, sliced
- 1 red onion, thinly sliced
- 2 tbsp olive oil
- Juice of 1 lime
- 1 tsp honey
- Salt and black pepper, to taste
- Fresh coriander, chopped, for garnish

Preparation instructions:
1. Preheat the Air Fryer to 200°C for 5 minutes.
2. In a bowl, toss prawns with 1 tablespoon of olive oil, salt, and black pepper.
3. Place the prawns in the Air Fryer basket. Air fry for 6 minutes or until the prawns are cooked through and golden.
4. In a large bowl, combine mixed salad greens, diced mango, sliced cucumber, and thinly sliced red onion.
5. In a small bowl, whisk together 1 tablespoon of olive oil, lime juice, honey, salt, and black pepper to make the dressing.
6. Drizzle the dressing over the salad and toss

to combine.
7. Top the salad with air-fried prawns and garnish with fresh coriander. Serve your Air-Fried Prawn and Mango Salad immediately.

Caprese Panini with Balsamic Glaze

Serves: 4 / Prep time: 10 minutes / Cook time: 5 minutes

Ingredients:
- 8 slices of ciabatta bread
- 2 large tomatoes, thinly sliced
- 200g fresh mozzarella cheese, sliced
- Fresh basil leaves
- 2 tbsp balsamic glaze
- 2 tbsp olive oil
- Salt and black pepper, to taste

Preparation instructions:
1. Preheat the Air Fryer to 180°C for 5 minutes.
2. Brush one side of each ciabatta slice with olive oil. On the non-oil-brushed side, layer tomato slices, mozzarella slices, and fresh basil leaves. Season with salt and black pepper.
3. Top with the remaining ciabatta slices to form sandwiches.
4. Place the sandwiches in the Air Fryer basket. Air fry for 5 minutes or until the bread is crispy and the cheese is melted.
5. Drizzle with balsamic glaze and serve your Caprese Panini with Balsamic Glaze hot.

Crispy Pork Schnitzel with Lemon Butter Sauce

Serves: 4 / Prep time: 20 minutes / Cook time: 10 minutes

Ingredients:
- 4 pork loin chops
- 100g plain flour
- 2 large eggs, beaten
- 150g breadcrumbs
- 2 tbsp olive oil
- Zest and juice of 1 lemon
- 2 tbsp butter
- Fresh parsley, chopped, for garnish
- Salt and black pepper, to taste

Preparation instructions:
1. Preheat the Air Fryer to 200°C for 5 minutes.
2. Season pork chops with salt and black pepper. Dredge each pork chop in flour, dip into beaten eggs, then coat with breadcrumbs.
3. Place the coated pork chops in the Air Fryer basket. Air fry for 10 minutes or until the pork is cooked through and golden brown.
4. In a small saucepan, melt butter over low heat. Add lemon zest and juice. Stir until well combined.
5. Drizzle the lemon butter sauce over the crispy pork schnitzel.
6. Garnish with fresh parsley and serve your Crispy Pork Schnitzel with Lemon Butter Sauce hot.

Air-Fried Vegetable and Chickpea Fritters

Serves: 4 / Prep time: 15 minutes / Cook time: 12 minutes

Ingredients:
- 200g chickpeas, drained and rinsed
- 1 courgette, grated
- 1 carrot, grated
- 1 small onion, finely chopped
- 2 cloves garlic, minced
- 2 tbsp fresh parsley, chopped
- 2 tbsp plain flour
- 1 tsp ground cumin
- 1/2 tsp baking powder
- Salt and black pepper, to taste
- Olive oil spray

Preparation instructions:
1. Preheat the Air Fryer to 190°C for 5 minutes.
2. In a large bowl, mash chickpeas with a fork. Add grated courgette, grated carrot, chopped onion, minced garlic, fresh parsley, plain flour, ground cumin, baking powder, salt, and black pepper. Mix until well combined.
3. Shape the mixture into small fritters.
4. Spray the Air Fryer basket with olive oil. Place the fritters in the basket in a single layer. Lightly spray the top of the fritters with olive oil.
5. Air fry for 12 minutes or until the fritters are golden and crispy.
6. Serve your Air-Fried Vegetable and Chickpea Fritters hot.

Chapter 4: Dinner Recipes

Crispy Air-Fried Chicken Thighs with Herbs

Serves: 4 / Prep time: 15 minutes / Cook time: 25 minutes

Ingredients:
- 4 chicken thighs, bone-in and skin-on
- 2 tbsp olive oil
- 1 tsp dried thyme
- 1 tsp dried rosemary
- Salt and black pepper, to taste

Preparation instructions:
1. Preheat the Air Fryer to 200°C for 5 minutes.
2. In a bowl, toss chicken thighs with olive oil, dried thyme, dried rosemary, salt, and black pepper.
3. Place the chicken thighs in the Air Fryer basket, skin side down. Air fry for 12 minutes.
4. Flip the chicken thighs, then air fry for an additional 13 minutes or until the skin is crispy and the chicken is cooked through.
5. Serve your Crispy Air-Fried Chicken Thighs with Herbs hot.

Air-Fried Lamb Chops with Mint Sauce

Serves: 4 / Prep time: 10 minutes / Cook time: 15 minutes

Ingredients:
- 4 lamb chops
- 2 tbsp olive oil
- 2 cloves garlic, minced
- 1 tsp dried mint
- Salt and black pepper, to taste

Preparation instructions:
1. Preheat the Air Fryer to 200°C for 5 minutes.
2. In a bowl, combine olive oil, minced garlic, dried mint, salt, and black pepper.
3. Coat the lamb chops with the olive oil mixture.
4. Place the lamb chops in the Air Fryer basket. Air fry for 15 minutes or until the lamb chops are cooked to your desired doneness.
5. Serve your Air-Fried Lamb Chops with Mint Sauce hot.

Vegetable and Chickpea Air-Fried Curry

Serves: 4 / Prep time: 15 minutes / Cook time: 20 minutes

Ingredients:
- 400g canned chickpeas, drained and rinsed
- 200g cauliflower florets
- 200g baby potatoes, halved
- 1 onion, finely chopped
- 2 cloves garlic, minced
- 1 tbsp curry powder
- 200ml coconut milk
- 2 tbsp olive oil
- Salt and black pepper, to taste
- Fresh coriander, chopped, for garnish

Preparation instructions:
1. Preheat the Air Fryer to 180°C for 5 minutes.
2. In a bowl, toss chickpeas, cauliflower florets, baby potatoes, chopped onion, minced garlic, curry powder, olive oil, salt, and black pepper.
3. Place the vegetable and chickpea mixture in the Air Fryer basket. Air fry for 20 minutes or until the vegetables are tender and golden.
4. Pour coconut milk over the cooked vegetables and chickpeas. Stir gently to combine.
5. Garnish with fresh coriander and serve your Vegetable and Chickpea Air-Fried Curry hot.

Teriyaki Salmon with Stir-Fried Vegetables

Serves: 4 / Prep time: 15 minutes / Cook time: 15 minutes

Ingredients:
- 4 salmon fillets
- 60ml teriyaki sauce
- 1 tbsp olive oil
- 200g broccoli florets
- 1 red pepper, sliced
- 1 yellow pepper, sliced
- 2 spring onions, sliced
- Sesame seeds, for garnish

Preparation instructions:
1. Preheat the Air Fryer to 200°C for 5 minutes.
2. Brush salmon fillets with teriyaki sauce.

3. In a separate bowl, toss broccoli florets, red pepper slices, yellow pepper slices, and spring onions with olive oil.
4. Place salmon fillets and the vegetable mixture in the Air Fryer basket. Air fry for 15 minutes or until the salmon is cooked through and the vegetables are tender.
5. Garnish with sesame seeds and serve your Teriyaki Salmon with Stir-Fried Vegetables hot.

Air-Fried Beef and Vegetable Stir Fry

Serves: 4 / Prep time: 15 minutes / Cook time: 10 minutes

Ingredients:
- 400g beef sirloin, thinly sliced
- 2 tbsp soy sauce
- 1 tbsp oyster sauce
- 1 tbsp olive oil
- 1 red onion, thinly sliced
- 1 carrot, julienned
- 1 green bell pepper, sliced
- 1 yellow bell pepper, sliced
- 2 cloves garlic, minced
- Fresh coriander, chopped, for garnish
- Sesame seeds, for garnish

Preparation instructions:
1. Preheat the Air Fryer to 200°C for 5 minutes.
2. In a bowl, marinate beef slices in soy sauce and oyster sauce for 10 minutes.
3. Heat olive oil in a pan over medium heat. Add marinated beef and cook until browned. Remove from the pan and set aside.
4. In the same pan, add a bit more oil if needed. Sauté red onion, julienned carrot, sliced green bell pepper, and sliced yellow bell pepper until tender. Add minced garlic and cook for an additional minute.
5. Place the cooked beef and vegetable mixture in the Air Fryer basket. Air fry for 10 minutes or until heated through.
6. Garnish with fresh coriander and sesame seeds. Serve your Air-Fried Beef and Vegetable Stir Fry hot.

Honey Garlic Air-Fried Pork Tenderloin

Serves: 4 / Prep time: 15 minutes / Cook time: 20 minutes

Ingredients:
- 500g pork tenderloin, trimmed
- 2 cloves garlic, minced
- 3 tbsp honey
- 2 tbsp soy sauce
- 1 tbsp olive oil
- Salt and black pepper, to taste
- Fresh parsley, chopped, for garnish

Preparation instructions:
1. Preheat the Air Fryer to 200°C for 5 minutes.
2. In a small bowl, mix minced garlic, honey, soy sauce, olive oil, salt, and black pepper.
3. Coat the pork tenderloin with the honey garlic marinade.
4. Place the marinated pork tenderloin in the Air Fryer basket. Air fry for 20 minutes or until the internal temperature reaches 70°C, turning halfway through the cooking time.
5. Let the pork rest for a few minutes, then slice. Garnish with fresh parsley and serve your Honey Garlic Air-Fried Pork Tenderloin hot.

Mediterranean Air-Fried Sea Bass

Serves: 4 / Prep time: 10 minutes / Cook time: 15 minutes

Ingredients:
- 4 sea bass fillets
- 2 tbsp olive oil
- 1 lemon, zested and juiced
- 2 cloves garlic, minced
- 1 tsp dried oregano
- Salt and black pepper, to taste
- Fresh parsley, chopped, for garnish

Preparation instructions:
1. Preheat the Air Fryer to 200°C for 5 minutes.
2. In a bowl, combine olive oil, lemon zest, lemon juice, minced garlic, dried oregano, salt, and black pepper.
3. Brush the sea bass fillets with the olive oil mixture.
4. Place the sea bass fillets in the Air Fryer basket. Air fry for 15 minutes or until the fish flakes easily with a fork.
5. Garnish with fresh parsley and serve your Mediterranean Air-Fried Sea Bass hot.

Air-Fried Pesto and Mozzarella Stuffed Chicken

Serves: 4 / Prep time: 15 minutes / Cook time: 25 minutes

Ingredients:
- 4 chicken breasts
- 4 tbsp pesto sauce
- 100g mozzarella cheese, sliced
- 1 tbsp olive oil
- Salt and black pepper, to taste
- Fresh basil leaves, for garnish

Preparation instructions:
1. Preheat the Air Fryer to 180°C for 5 minutes.
2. Cut a pocket horizontally into each chicken breast.
3. Spread 1 tablespoon of pesto inside each pocket and stuff with mozzarella slices.
4. Brush the stuffed chicken breasts with olive oil, then season with salt and black pepper.
5. Place the stuffed chicken breasts in the Air Fryer basket. Air fry for 25 minutes or until the internal temperature reaches 75°C.
6. Garnish with fresh basil leaves and serve your Air-Fried Pesto and Mozzarella Stuffed Chicken hot.

Crispy Coconut-Crusted Tofu with Sweet Chilli Sauce

Serves: 4 / Prep time: 20 minutes / Cook time: 15 minutes

Ingredients:
- 400g firm tofu, pressed and cut into cubes
- 100g desiccated coconut
- 2 tbsp cornstarch
- 1/2 tsp garlic powder
- Salt and black pepper, to taste
- 150ml sweet chilli sauce

Preparation instructions:
1. Preheat the Air Fryer to 180°C for 5 minutes.
2. In a bowl, combine desiccated coconut, cornstarch, garlic powder, salt, and black pepper.
3. Roll tofu cubes in the coconut mixture, pressing gently to adhere.
4. Place the coated tofu cubes in the Air Fryer basket. Air fry for 15 minutes or until golden and crispy, turning halfway through the cooking time.
5. Serve your Crispy Coconut-Crusted Tofu with Sweet Chilli Sauce for dipping.

Air-Fried Sausages with Onion Gravy

Serves: 4 / Prep time: 10 minutes / Cook time: 20 minutes

Ingredients:
- 8 sausages
- 2 onions, thinly sliced
- 2 tbsp olive oil
- 1 tbsp plain flour
- 300ml beef stock
- Salt and black pepper, to taste

Preparation instructions:
1. Preheat the Air Fryer to 200°C for 5 minutes.
2. Place sausages in the Air Fryer basket. Air fry for 20 minutes or until cooked through, turning occasionally.
3. In a pan, heat olive oil over medium heat. Add thinly sliced onions and cook until golden brown.
4. Stir in plain flour, then slowly pour in beef stock, stirring continuously until the gravy thickens.
5. Season with salt and black pepper. Serve your Air-Fried Sausages with Onion Gravy hot, drizzled with the gravy.

Lemon Herb Air-Fried Cod Fillets

Serves: 4 / Prep time: 10 minutes / Cook time: 12 minutes

Ingredients:
- 4 cod fillets, 150g each
- Zest and juice of 1 lemon
- 2 tbsp fresh parsley, finely chopped
- 1 tbsp olive oil
- Salt and black pepper, to taste

Preparation instructions:
1. Preheat the Air Fryer to 190°C for 5 minutes.
2. In a bowl, combine lemon zest, lemon juice, fresh parsley, olive oil, salt, and black pepper.
3. Coat the cod fillets with the lemon herb mixture.
4. Place the coated cod fillets in the Air Fryer basket. Air fry for 12 minutes or until the fish flakes easily with a fork.
5. Serve your Lemon Herb Air-Fried Cod Fillets hot, garnished with extra fresh parsley.

Air-Fried Vegetable and Paneer Skewers

Serves: 4 / Prep time: 15 minutes / Cook time: 10 minutes

Ingredients:
- 200g paneer, cubed
- 1 red pepper, cut into chunks

- 1 yellow pepper, cut into chunks
- 1 red onion, cut into chunks
- 2 tbsp olive oil
- 1 tsp cumin powder
- 1/2 tsp paprika
- Salt and black pepper, to taste

Preparation instructions:
1. Preheat the Air Fryer to 180°C for 5 minutes.
2. In a bowl, toss paneer, red pepper, yellow pepper, and red onion with olive oil, cumin powder, paprika, salt, and black pepper.
3. Thread the marinated paneer and vegetables onto skewers.
4. Place the skewers in the Air Fryer basket. Air fry for 10 minutes or until the vegetables are tender and slightly charred, turning halfway through the cooking time.
5. Serve your Air-Fried Vegetable and Paneer Skewers hot, accompanied by your favourite dipping sauce.

Crispy Air-Fried Duck Breast with Orange Glaze

Serves: 4 / Prep time: 15 minutes / Cook time: 20 minutes

Ingredients:
- 4 duck breast fillets
- Salt and black pepper, to taste
- 2 tbsp olive oil
- 4 tbsp orange marmalade
- 2 tbsp soy sauce
- Zest and juice of 1 orange

Preparation instructions:
1. Preheat the Air Fryer to 180°C for 5 minutes.
2. Score the duck skin in a crosshatch pattern and season with salt and black pepper.
3. Heat olive oil in a pan over medium-high heat. Sear the duck breast fillets, skin side down, until golden brown and crispy, about 4-5 minutes per side.
4. In a small saucepan, combine orange marmalade, soy sauce, orange zest, and orange juice. Heat over low heat, stirring, until the glaze thickens slightly.
5. Brush the seared duck breasts with the orange glaze.
6. Place the glazed duck breasts in the Air Fryer basket. Air fry for 20 minutes or until cooked to your desired doneness, brushing with additional glaze halfway through the cooking time.
7. Rest the duck for a few minutes, then slice. Serve your Crispy Air-Fried Duck Breast with Orange Glaze hot.

Air-Fried Beef and Mushroom Pie

Serves: 4 / Prep time: 20 minutes / Cook time: 18 minutes

Ingredients:
- 400g beef steak, diced
- 200g mushrooms, sliced
- 1 onion, finely chopped
- 2 tbsp olive oil
- 2 tbsp plain flour
- 300ml beef stock
- Salt and black pepper, to taste
- 500g puff pastry, thawed if frozen
- 1 egg, beaten, for egg wash

Preparation instructions:
1. Preheat the Air Fryer to 200°C for 5 minutes.
2. Heat olive oil in a pan over medium heat. Add diced beef, mushrooms, and chopped onion. Cook until the beef is browned and the vegetables are tender.
3. Stir in plain flour, then slowly pour in beef stock, stirring continuously until the filling thickens. Season with salt and black pepper. Let the filling cool.
4. Roll out the puff pastry and cut out 4 circles for pie lids and 4 smaller circles for bases.
5. Place the smaller pastry circles into the base of 4 silicone muffin cups.
6. Fill each cup with the cooled beef and mushroom mixture.
7. Cover the filling with the larger pastry circles, pressing the edges to seal.
8. Brush the pastry tops with beaten egg.
9. Place the muffin cups in the Air Fryer basket. Air fry for 18 minutes or until the pastry is golden brown and crisp.
10. Let the pies cool for a few minutes before serving your Air-Fried Beef and Mushroom Pie.

Stuffed Peppers with Quinoa and Cheese

Serves: 4 / Prep time: 20 minutes / Cook time:

20 minutes

Ingredients:
- 4 large peppers, any colour
- 150g quinoa, cooked according to package instructions
- 1 tsp cumin powder
- 100g cheddar cheese, grated
- 1 can (400g) black beans, drained and rinsed
- Salt and black pepper, to taste
- Fresh coriander, chopped, for garnish

Preparation instructions:
1. Preheat the Air Fryer to 180°C for 5 minutes.
2. Cut the tops off the peppers and remove the seeds and membranes.
3. In a bowl, combine cooked quinoa, grated cheddar cheese, black beans, cumin powder, salt, and black pepper.
4. Stuff the peppers with the quinoa mixture.
5. Place the stuffed peppers in the Air Fryer basket. Air fry for 20 minutes or until the peppers are tender and the filling is heated through.
6. Garnish with fresh coriander and serve your Stuffed Peppers with Quinoa and Cheese hot.

Air-Fried Butter Chicken with Naan Bread

Serves: 4 / Prep time: 15 minutes / Cook time: 20 minutes

Ingredients:
- 500g boneless, skinless chicken thighs, cut into bite-sized pieces
- 1 onion, finely chopped
- 2 cloves garlic, minced
- 1-inch ginger, grated
- 1 tsp garam masala
- 1 tsp ground turmeric
- 1 tsp ground cumin
- 1 tsp ground coriander
- 1/2 tsp chilli powder
- 1/2 tsp paprika
- 1/4 tsp cinnamon
- 200g canned tomato sauce
- 150ml double cream
- 60g unsalted butter
- Salt and black pepper, to taste
- Fresh coriander, chopped, for garnish
- Naan bread, to serve

Preparation instructions:
1. Preheat the Air Fryer to 180°C for 5 minutes.
2. In a pan, melt 30g of butter. Add chopped onion, minced garlic, and grated ginger. Sauté until the onion is translucent.
3. Add garam masala, ground turmeric, ground cumin, ground coriander, chilli powder, paprika, and cinnamon. Cook for 2-3 minutes until fragrant.
4. Add chicken pieces and cook until they are browned on all sides.
5. Stir in the canned tomato sauce and double cream. Simmer for 10 minutes until the sauce thickens. Season with salt and black pepper.
6. In another pan, melt the remaining 30g of butter. Toast the naan bread on both sides until golden brown.
7. Serve the Air-Fried Butter Chicken hot, garnished with fresh coriander, with warm naan bread on the side.

Air-Fried BBQ Pork Ribs

Serves: 4 / Prep time: 15 minutes / Cook time: 25 minutes

Ingredients:
- 800g pork ribs
- 200ml BBQ sauce
- 2 tbsp honey
- 1 tbsp Worcestershire sauce
- 1 tsp smoked paprika
- 1/2 tsp garlic powder
- 1/2 tsp onion powder
- Salt and black pepper, to taste

Preparation instructions:
1. Preheat the Air Fryer to 180°C for 5 minutes.
2. In a bowl, combine BBQ sauce, honey, Worcestershire sauce, smoked paprika, garlic powder, onion powder, salt, and black pepper.
3. Coat the pork ribs with the BBQ sauce mixture.
4. Place the coated pork ribs in the Air Fryer basket. Air fry for 25 minutes, turning halfway through the cooking time, until the ribs are cooked through and caramelised.
5. Serve the Air-Fried BBQ Pork Ribs hot.

Crispy Air-Fried Falafel Platter

Serves: 4 / Prep time: 20 minutes / Cook time: 15 minutes

Ingredients:
- 400g canned chickpeas, drained and rinsed
- 1 small onion, chopped
- 2 cloves garlic, minced

- 2 tbsp fresh parsley, chopped
- 1 tsp ground cumin
- 1/2 tsp ground coriander
- 1/4 tsp cayenne pepper
- Salt and black pepper, to taste
- 2 tbsp plain flour
- 2 tbsp olive oil, for brushing
- Hummus, tahini sauce, and pita bread, to serve

Preparation instructions:
1. Preheat the Air Fryer to 180°C for 5 minutes.
2. In a food processor, combine chickpeas, chopped onion, minced garlic, fresh parsley, ground cumin, ground coriander, cayenne pepper, salt, black pepper, and plain flour. Blend until a coarse mixture forms.
3. Shape the mixture into small falafel balls.
4. Brush the falafel balls with olive oil and place them in the Air Fryer basket. Air fry for 15 minutes, turning halfway through, until the falafels are crispy and golden brown.
5. Serve the Crispy Air-Fried Falafel hot, accompanied by hummus, tahini sauce, and warm pita bread.

Air-Fried Shrimp Scampi with Linguine

Serves: 4 / Prep time: 15 minutes / Cook time: 10 minutes

Ingredients:
- 400g large shrimp, peeled and deveined
- 250g linguine, cooked according to package instructions
- 4 cloves garlic, minced
- Zest and juice of 1 lemon
- 1/4 tsp red pepper flakes
- 60ml white wine
- 2 tbsp fresh parsley, chopped
- 2 tbsp olive oil
- Salt and black pepper, to taste
- Grated Parmesan cheese, for garnish

Preparation instructions:
1. Preheat the Air Fryer to 180°C for 5 minutes.
2. In a bowl, combine shrimp, minced garlic, lemon zest, red pepper flakes, salt, and black pepper.
3. Heat olive oil in a pan over medium heat. Add the shrimp mixture and cook until the shrimp turn pink, about 2-3 minutes.
4. Deglaze the pan with white wine and lemon juice. Cook for another 2 minutes.
5. Toss the cooked linguine with the shrimp mixture.
6. Garnish with fresh parsley and grated Parmesan cheese before serving your Air-Fried Shrimp Scampi with Linguine.

Air-Fried Vegetable and Lentil Curry

Serves: 4 / Prep time: 15 minutes / Cook time: 20 minutes

Ingredients:
- 200g red lentils, cooked
- 1 onion, chopped
- 2 cloves garlic, minced
- 1-inch ginger, grated
- 400ml coconut milk
- 200ml vegetable stock
- 1 tbsp curry powder
- 1 tsp ground turmeric
- 1 tsp ground cumin
- 1 tsp ground coriander
- 1 tbsp vegetable oil
- Salt and black pepper, to taste
- Fresh coriander, chopped, for garnish
- Steamed rice, to serve

Preparation instructions:
1. Preheat the Air Fryer to 180°C for 5 minutes.
2. In a pan, heat vegetable oil over medium heat. Add chopped onion, minced garlic, and grated ginger. Sauté until the onion is translucent.
3. Add curry powder, ground turmeric, ground cumin, and ground coriander. Cook for 2-3 minutes until fragrant.
4. Pour in coconut milk and vegetable stock. Stir well.
5. Add cooked red lentils to the curry mixture. Simmer for 10 minutes until the flavours meld together. Season with salt and black pepper.
6. Garnish with fresh coriander and serve the Air-Fried Vegetable and Lentil Curry hot with steamed rice.

Chapter 5: Vegetable and Vegetarian Recipes

Crispy Air-Fried Vegetable Spring Rolls

Serves: 4 / Prep time: 20 minutes / Cook time: 15 minutes

Ingredients:
- 200g bean sprouts
- 150g shredded cabbage
- 100g julienned carrots
- 1 red pepper, thinly sliced
- 2 spring onions, finely chopped
- 1 clove garlic, minced
- 1 tsp grated ginger
- 2 tbsp soy sauce
- 1 tbsp sesame oil
- 12 spring roll wrappers
- 2 tbsp vegetable oil, for brushing
- Sweet chilli sauce, for dipping

Preparation instructions:
1. Preheat the Air Fryer to 190°C for 5 minutes.
2. In a pan, heat sesame oil over medium heat. Add garlic and grated ginger, sauté until fragrant.
3. Add bean sprouts, shredded cabbage, julienned carrots, sliced red pepper, and chopped spring onions. Stir-fry for 2-3 minutes. Add soy sauce and toss until the vegetables are tender. Remove from heat and let the mixture cool.
4. Place a spoonful of the vegetable filling on a spring roll wrapper. Fold the sides and roll tightly. Seal the edge with water.
5. Brush the spring rolls with vegetable oil and place them in the Air Fryer basket. Air fry for 15 minutes, turning halfway through, until golden and crispy.
6. Serve the Crispy Air-Fried Vegetable Spring Rolls hot, with sweet chilli sauce for dipping.

Stuffed Portobello Mushrooms with Spinach and Feta

Serves: 4 / Prep time: 15 minutes / Cook time: 15 minutes

Ingredients:
- 4 large Portobello mushrooms, stems removed and cleaned
- 200g fresh spinach, chopped
- 100g crumbled feta cheese
- 2 cloves garlic, minced
- 1 tbsp olive oil
- Salt and black pepper, to taste
- Fresh parsley, chopped, for garnish

Preparation instructions:
1. Preheat the Air Fryer to 190°C for 5 minutes.
2. In a pan, heat olive oil over medium heat. Add minced garlic and chopped spinach. Sauté until the spinach wilts.
3. Remove the pan from heat and stir in crumbled feta cheese. Season with salt and black pepper.
4. Stuff the Portobello mushrooms with the spinach and feta mixture.
5. Place the stuffed mushrooms in the Air Fryer basket. Air fry for 15 minutes until the mushrooms are tender.
6. Garnish with fresh parsley before serving the Stuffed Portobello Mushrooms hot.

Air-Fried Sweet Potato Wedges with Rosemary

Serves: 4 / Prep time: 10 minutes / Cook time: 20 minutes

Ingredients:
- 2 large sweet potatoes, peeled and cut into wedges
- 2 tbsp olive oil
- 1 tsp dried rosemary
- Salt and black pepper, to taste

Preparation instructions:
1. Preheat the Air Fryer to 190°C for 5 minutes.
2. In a bowl, toss sweet potato wedges with olive oil, dried rosemary, salt, and black pepper until evenly coated.
3. Place the sweet potato wedges in the Air Fryer basket. Air fry for 20 minutes, shaking the basket halfway through, until the wedges are crispy and golden brown.
4. Serve the Air-Fried Sweet Potato Wedges hot.

Spicy Air-Fried Cauliflower Bites

Serves: 4 / Prep time: 15 minutes / Cook time: 20 minutes

Ingredients:
- 1 medium cauliflower, cut into florets

- 100g plain flour
- 1 tsp smoked paprika
- 1/2 tsp garlic powder
- 1/2 tsp onion powder
- 1/4 tsp cayenne pepper
- 120ml water
- 2 tbsp hot sauce
- Salt and black pepper, to taste
- 1 tbsp unsalted butter, melted
- Fresh parsley, chopped, for garnish

Preparation instructions:
1. Preheat the Air Fryer to 190°C for 5 minutes.
2. In a bowl, whisk together plain flour, smoked paprika, garlic powder, onion powder, cayenne pepper, water, salt, and black pepper to make the batter.
3. Dip cauliflower florets into the batter, coating them evenly, and place them in the Air Fryer basket.
4. Air fry for 20 minutes, turning halfway through, until the cauliflower is crispy and golden brown.
5. In a separate bowl, combine hot sauce and melted butter. Toss the air-fried cauliflower in the spicy sauce mixture.
6. Garnish with fresh parsley before serving the Spicy Air-Fried Cauliflower Bites hot.

Crispy Halloumi Fries with Yoghurt Dip

Serves: 4 / Prep time: 10 minutes / Cook time: 15 minutes

Ingredients:
- 250g halloumi cheese, cut into fries
- 50g plain flour
- 1/2 tsp smoked paprika
- 1/2 tsp garlic powder
- 1/4 tsp cayenne pepper
- Salt and black pepper, to taste
- 1 egg, beaten
- 100g breadcrumbs
- Vegetable oil, for brushing
- 200g Greek yoghurt
- Fresh mint, chopped, for garnish

Preparation instructions:
1. Preheat the Air Fryer to 200°C for 5 minutes.
2. In a bowl, combine plain flour, smoked paprika, garlic powder, cayenne pepper, salt, and black pepper.
3. Dip halloumi fries into the flour mixture, then into beaten egg, and finally into breadcrumbs, pressing gently to adhere.
4. Place the halloumi fries in the Air Fryer basket. Air fry for 15 minutes, turning halfway through, until crispy and golden brown.
5. In a small bowl, mix Greek yoghurt with chopped fresh mint to make the dip.
6. Serve the Crispy Halloumi Fries hot, with the yoghurt dip on the side.

Air-Fried Mediterranean Stuffed Peppers

Serves: 4 / Prep time: 15 minutes / Cook time: 25 minutes

Ingredients:
- 4 large peppers (any colour)
- 200g cooked quinoa
- 100g cherry tomatoes, halved
- 60g Kalamata olives, pitted and chopped
- 60g crumbled feta cheese
- 2 tbsp chopped fresh parsley
- 1 tbsp olive oil
- 1/2 tsp dried oregano
- Salt and black pepper, to taste

Preparation instructions:
1. Preheat the Air Fryer to 190°C for 5 minutes.
2. Cut the tops off the peppers and remove the seeds and membranes.
3. In a bowl, combine cooked quinoa, cherry tomatoes, Kalamata olives, crumbled feta cheese, chopped fresh parsley, olive oil, dried oregano, salt, and black pepper.
4. Stuff the peppers with the quinoa mixture.
5. Place the stuffed peppers in the Air Fryer basket. Air fry for 25 minutes, until the peppers are tender and slightly charred.
6. Serve the Air-Fried Mediterranean Stuffed Peppers hot.

Air-Fried Veggie Burger Patties

Makes: 4 patties / Prep time: 15 minutes / Cook time: 20 minutes

Ingredients:
- 400g mixed canned beans (such as black beans, chickpeas), drained and rinsed
- 1 small red onion, finely chopped
- 1 garlic clove, minced

- 1 tsp ground cumin • 1 tsp paprika
- Salt and black pepper, to taste
- 60g breadcrumbs • 1 egg, beaten
- 2 tbsp olive oil

Preparation instructions:
1. Preheat the Air Fryer to 190°C for 5 minutes.
2. In a bowl, mash the mixed beans with a fork or potato masher.
3. Add chopped red onion, minced garlic, ground cumin, paprika, salt, black pepper, breadcrumbs, and beaten egg to the mashed beans. Mix until well combined.
4. Shape the mixture into 4 patties.
5. Brush the patties with olive oil and place them in the Air Fryer basket. Air fry for 20 minutes, turning halfway through, until the patties are golden and crispy.
6. Serve the Air-Fried Veggie Burger Patties hot, in burger buns with your favourite toppings.

Panko-Crusted Air-Fried Courgette Chips

Serves: 4 / Prep time: 15 minutes / Cook time: 15 minutes

Ingredients:
- 2 large courgettes, sliced into 1/4-inch thick rounds
- 60g plain flour • 2 eggs, beaten
- 120g panko breadcrumbs
- 1/2 tsp dried basil • 1/2 tsp garlic powder
- 1/2 tsp onion powder • Olive oil spray
- Salt and black pepper, to taste

Preparation instructions:
1. Preheat the Air Fryer to 190°C for 5 minutes.
2. In separate bowls, place plain flour, beaten eggs, and a mixture of panko breadcrumbs, dried basil, garlic powder, onion powder, salt, and black pepper.
3. Dip courgette slices first in flour, then in beaten eggs, and finally coat with the panko mixture.
4. Place the coated courgette slices in the Air Fryer basket. Lightly spray with olive oil.
5. Air fry for 15 minutes, turning halfway through, until the courgette chips are crispy and golden brown.
6. Serve the Panko-Crusted Air-Fried Courgette Chips hot, with a dipping sauce of your choice.

Air-Fried Asparagus Spears with Lemon Zest

Serves: 4 / Prep time: 10 minutes / Cook time: 10 minutes

Ingredients:
- 300g fresh asparagus spears, trimmed
- 1 tbsp olive oil • Zest of 1 lemon
- Salt and black pepper, to taste

Preparation instructions:
1. Preheat the Air Fryer to 190°C for 5 minutes.
2. Toss asparagus spears with olive oil, lemon zest, salt, and black pepper.
3. Place the asparagus spears in the Air Fryer basket. Air fry for 10 minutes, until tender-crisp and slightly charred.
4. Serve the Air-Fried Asparagus Spears with Lemon Zest hot.

Stuffed Butternut Squash with Quinoa and Cranberries

Serves: 4 / Prep time: 15 minutes / Cook time: 40 minutes

Ingredients:
- 2 small butternut squashes, halved and seeds removed
- 200g cooked quinoa • 60g dried cranberries
- 60g chopped nuts (such as almonds or pecans)
- 1 tbsp olive oil • 1/2 tsp ground cinnamon
- Salt and black pepper, to taste
- Fresh parsley, chopped, for garnish

Preparation instructions:
1. Preheat the Air Fryer to 190°C for 5 minutes.
2. Scoop out a portion of the flesh from each butternut squash half to create a hollow space for the filling.
3. In a bowl, combine cooked quinoa, dried cranberries, chopped nuts, olive oil, ground cinnamon, salt, and black pepper.
4. Stuff the butternut squash halves with the quinoa mixture.
5. Place the stuffed squash halves in the Air

Fryer basket. Air fry for 40 minutes, until the squash is tender.
6. Garnish with fresh parsley before serving the Stuffed Butternut Squash with Quinoa and Cranberries hot.

Air-Fried Brussels Sprouts with Balsamic Glaze

Serves: 4 / Prep time: 10 minutes / Cook time: 15 minutes

Ingredients:
- 400g Brussels sprouts, trimmed and halved
- 30ml olive oil
- Salt and black pepper, to taste
- 60ml balsamic glaze

Preparation instructions:
1. Preheat the Air Fryer to 190°C for 5 minutes.
2. In a bowl, toss Brussels sprouts with olive oil, salt, and black pepper until evenly coated.
3. Place Brussels sprouts in the Air Fryer basket. Air fry for 15 minutes, shaking the basket halfway through, until crispy and golden brown.
4. Drizzle with balsamic glaze before serving the Air-Fried Brussels Sprouts hot.

Air-Fried Vegetable Tempura with Dipping Sauce

Serves: 4 / Prep time: 15 minutes / Cook time: 10 minutes

Ingredients:
- For the tempura:
- 200g broccoli florets
- 200g sweet potato, thinly sliced
- 200g courgette, thinly sliced
- 100g plain flour
- 1/2 tsp baking powder
- 1/4 tsp salt
- 200ml cold water
- Vegetable oil, for frying
- For the dipping sauce:
- 60ml soy sauce
- 30ml rice vinegar
- 1 tbsp honey
- 1/2 tsp grated fresh ginger
- 1 green onion, finely chopped

Preparation instructions:
1. Preheat the Air Fryer to 190°C for 5 minutes.
2. In a bowl, whisk together plain flour, baking powder, salt, and cold water until you get a smooth batter.
3. Dip broccoli, sweet potato, and courgette slices into the batter, ensuring they are well coated.
4. Place the battered vegetables in the Air Fryer basket. Air fry for 10 minutes, until the tempura is crispy and golden brown.
5. While the tempura is cooking, prepare the dipping sauce by mixing soy sauce, rice vinegar, honey, grated fresh ginger, and chopped green onion.
6. Serve the Air-Fried Vegetable Tempura hot with the dipping sauce.

Crispy Air-Fried Tofu Nuggets

Serves: 4 / Prep time: 20 minutes / Cook time: 15 minutes

Ingredients:
- 400g firm tofu, pressed and cut into bite-sized cubes
- 60g cornstarch
- 1/2 tsp garlic powder
- 1/2 tsp paprika
- Salt and black pepper, to taste
- Vegetable oil spray

Preparation instructions:
1. Preheat the Air Fryer to 190°C for 5 minutes.
2. In a bowl, mix cornstarch, garlic powder, paprika, salt, and black pepper.
3. Toss tofu cubes in the cornstarch mixture, ensuring they are well coated.
4. Place the coated tofu cubes in the Air Fryer basket. Lightly spray with vegetable oil.
5. Air fry for 15 minutes, shaking the basket halfway through, until the tofu nuggets are crispy and golden brown.
6. Serve the Crispy Air-Fried Tofu Nuggets hot, with your favourite dipping sauce.

Air-Fried Ratatouille with Herbs de Provence

Serves: 4 / Prep time: 20 minutes / Cook time: 25 minutes

Ingredients:
- 1 large aubergine, diced
- 2 medium courgettes, diced
- 2 red peppers, diced
- 1 onion, finely chopped
- 2 tbsp olive oil
- 2 garlic cloves, minced

- 1 tsp Herbs de Provence
- Salt and black pepper, to taste
- 400g canned chopped tomatoes
- Fresh basil leaves, for garnish

Preparation instructions:
1. Preheat the Air Fryer to 190°C for 5 minutes.
2. In a large bowl, combine diced aubergine, courgettes, red bell peppers, and finely chopped onion.
3. Drizzle olive oil over the vegetables, add minced garlic, Herbs de Provence, salt, and black pepper. Toss to coat evenly.
4. Place the seasoned vegetables in the Air Fryer basket. Air fry for 25 minutes, shaking the basket occasionally, until the vegetables are tender and slightly charred.
5. Stir in canned chopped tomatoes and air fry for an additional 5 minutes.
6. Garnish the Air-Fried Ratatouille with fresh basil leaves before serving.

Sweet and Spicy Air-Fried Carrots

Serves: 4 / Prep time: 10 minutes / Cook time: 15 minutes

Ingredients:
- 400g baby carrots, halved lengthwise
- 30ml honey
- 15ml soy sauce
- 1/2 tsp Sriracha sauce
- 1/2 tsp sesame oil
- 1/2 tsp grated fresh ginger
- Sesame seeds, for garnish
- Fresh coriander leaves, for garnish

Preparation instructions:
1. Preheat the Air Fryer to 190°C for 5 minutes.
2. In a bowl, whisk together honey, soy sauce, Sriracha sauce, sesame oil, and grated fresh ginger.
3. Toss halved baby carrots in the sauce mixture, ensuring they are well coated.
4. Place the carrots in the Air Fryer basket. Air fry for 15 minutes, shaking the basket occasionally, until the carrots are tender and caramelised.
5. Garnish the Sweet and Spicy Air-Fried Carrots with sesame seeds and fresh coriander leaves before serving hot.

Air-Fried Chickpea and Spinach Falafel

Serves: 4 / Prep time: 15 minutes / Cook time: 15 minutes

Ingredients:
- 400g canned chickpeas, drained and rinsed
- 100g fresh spinach, finely chopped
- 1 small onion, finely chopped
- 2 cloves garlic, minced
- 1 tsp ground cumin
- 1 tsp ground coriander
- 1/2 tsp ground turmeric
- Salt and black pepper, to taste
- 30g breadcrumbs
- 1 egg, beaten
- Vegetable oil spray

Preparation instructions:
1. Preheat the Air Fryer to 190°C for 5 minutes.
2. In a food processor, combine chickpeas, spinach, onion, garlic, cumin, coriander, turmeric, salt, and black pepper. Pulse until well combined but not completely smooth.
3. Transfer the mixture to a bowl. Stir in breadcrumbs and beaten egg until the mixture holds together.
4. Shape the mixture into small falafel balls.
5. Place the falafel balls in the Air Fryer basket. Lightly spray with vegetable oil.
6. Air fry for 15 minutes, turning halfway through, until the falafel is crispy and golden brown.
7. Serve the Air-Fried Chickpea and Spinach Falafel hot, with your favourite dipping sauce.

Air-Fried Stuffed Mushrooms with Herbs

Serves: 4 / Prep time: 10 minutes / Cook time: 12 minutes

Ingredients:
- 8 large button mushrooms, stems removed and finely chopped
- 50g cream cheese
- 1 tbsp grated Parmesan cheese
- 1 clove garlic, minced
- 1 tbsp fresh parsley, chopped
- Salt and black pepper, to taste
- Vegetable oil spray

Preparation instructions:
1. Preheat the Air Fryer to 190°C for 5 minutes.
2. In a bowl, combine chopped mushroom stems, cream cheese, Parmesan cheese, minced garlic, fresh parsley, salt, and black pepper. Mix until well combined.

3. Stuff the mushroom caps with the cream cheese mixture.
4. Place the stuffed mushrooms in the Air Fryer basket. Lightly spray with vegetable oil.
5. Air fry for 12 minutes, until the mushrooms are tender and the filling is golden and bubbly.
6. Serve the Air-Fried Stuffed Mushrooms hot, garnished with additional chopped parsley if desired.

Crispy Air-Fried Aubergine Slices

Serves: 4 / Prep time: 15 minutes / Cook time: 15 minutes

Ingredients:
- 1 large aubergine, sliced into 1 cm thick rounds
- 60g plain flour
- 2 eggs, beaten
- 100g breadcrumbs
- 1 tsp dried oregano
- 1/2 tsp garlic powder
- Vegetable oil spray
- Salt and black pepper, to taste

Preparation instructions:
1. Preheat the Air Fryer to 190°C for 5 minutes.
2. In separate bowls, place flour, beaten eggs, and a mixture of breadcrumbs, dried oregano, garlic powder, salt, and black pepper.
3. Dip aubergine slices first in flour, then in eggs, and finally in the breadcrumb mixture, pressing gently to adhere.
4. Place the breaded aubergine slices in the Air Fryer basket. Lightly spray with vegetable oil.
5. Air fry for 15 minutes, turning halfway through, until the aubergine is crispy and golden brown.
6. Serve the Crispy Air-Fried aubergine Slices hot, with marinara sauce for dipping.

Air-Fried Sesame-Ginger Broccoli Florets

Serves: 4 / Prep time: 10 minutes / Cook time: 8 minutes

Ingredients:
- 400g broccoli florets
- 30ml soy sauce
- 15ml honey
- 1 tbsp sesame oil
- 1 clove garlic, minced
- 1 tsp grated fresh ginger
- 1 tbsp sesame seeds, for garnish

Preparation instructions:
1. Preheat the Air Fryer to 190°C for 5 minutes.
2. In a bowl, whisk together soy sauce, honey, sesame oil, minced garlic, and grated fresh ginger.
3. Toss broccoli florets in the sauce mixture until well coated.
4. Place the coated broccoli florets in the Air Fryer basket. Air fry for 8 minutes, shaking the basket occasionally, until the broccoli is tender-crisp.
5. Garnish the Air-Fried Sesame-Ginger Broccoli Florets with sesame seeds before serving hot.

Air-Fried Veggie Kebabs with Tzatziki Sauce

Serves: 4 / Prep time: 15 minutes / Cook time: 10 minutes

Ingredients:
- 1 red pepper, cut into chunks
- 1 yellow pepper, cut into chunks
- 1 courgette, sliced into rounds
- 1 red onion, cut into wedges
- 1 tbsp olive oil
- Salt and black pepper, to taste
- 4 wooden skewers, soaked in water for 30 minutes
- Fresh parsley, for garnish
- Tzatziki Sauce:
- 150g Greek yoghurt
- 1/2 cucumber, grated and squeezed to remove excess moisture
- 1 clove garlic, minced
- 1 tbsp fresh dill, chopped
- 1 tbsp lemon juice
- Salt and black pepper, to taste

Preparation instructions:
1. Preheat the Air Fryer to 190°C for 5 minutes.
2. In a bowl, toss the peppers, courgette, and red onion with olive oil, salt, and black pepper.
3. Thread the vegetables onto the soaked wooden skewers, alternating the colours.
4. Place the vegetable kebabs in the Air Fryer basket. Air fry for 10 minutes, turning halfway through, until the vegetables are tender and slightly charred.
5. In a separate bowl, combine Greek yoghurt, grated cucumber, minced garlic, fresh dill, lemon juice, salt, and black pepper to make the tzatziki sauce.
6. Serve the Air-Fried Veggie Kebabs hot, garnished with fresh parsley and accompanied by tzatziki sauce for dipping.

Chapter 6: Sides and Appetisers Recipes

Crispy Air-Fried Potato Skins with Cheddar and Bacon

Serves: 4 / Prep time: 15 minutes / Cook time: 20 minutes

Ingredients:
- 4 medium potatoes, scrubbed clean
- 120g shredded cheddar cheese
- 4 slices bacon, cooked and crumbled
- 2 spring onions, finely chopped
- 15ml vegetable oil
- Salt and black pepper, to taste
- Sour cream, for serving
- Fresh chives, chopped, for garnish

Preparation instructions:
1. Preheat the Air Fryer to 200°C for 5 minutes.
2. Pierce each potato several times with a fork. Rub potatoes with vegetable oil and season with salt.
3. Air fry the potatoes for 40-45 minutes or until tender. Let cool slightly.
4. Cut the potatoes in half lengthwise. Scoop out the flesh, leaving about 1cm of potato attached to the skin.
5. Brush the inside and outside of the potato skins with vegetable oil. Air fry for 10 minutes or until crisp.
6. Remove from the Air Fryer. Fill each skin with shredded cheddar cheese and crumbled bacon.
7. Return to the Air Fryer and air fry for another 5 minutes or until the cheese is melted and bubbly.
8. Remove from the Air Fryer and sprinkle with chopped spring onions and black pepper. Serve with sour cream and garnish with fresh chives.

Air-Fried Mac and Cheese Bites with Sriracha Mayo

Serves: 4 / Prep time: 20 minutes / Cook time: 15 minutes

Ingredients:
- 200g macaroni, cooked and cooled
- 120g shredded cheddar cheese
- 60g grated Parmesan cheese
- 1 egg, beaten
- 30ml whole milk
- Salt and black pepper, to taste
- 50g plain flour
- 75g panko breadcrumbs
- Vegetable oil spray
- 60ml mayonnaise
- 1-2 tsp Sriracha sauce, to taste

Preparation instructions:
1. Preheat the Air Fryer to 200°C for 5 minutes.
2. In a bowl, combine macaroni, shredded cheddar cheese, grated Parmesan cheese, beaten egg, milk, salt, and black pepper. Mix well.
3. Shape the mixture into bite-sized balls.
4. Place the flour and panko breadcrumbs in separate bowls.
5. Roll each mac and cheese ball in flour, dip in beaten egg, and coat with panko breadcrumbs.
6. Arrange the coated balls in the Air Fryer basket. Lightly spray with vegetable oil.
7. Air fry for 12-15 minutes or until golden and crispy.
8. In a small bowl, mix mayonnaise and Sriracha sauce to make the dipping sauce.
9. Serve the Air-Fried Mac and Cheese Bites hot, with Sriracha mayo on the side for dipping.

Parmesan and Garlic Air-Fried Green Beans

Serves: 4 / Prep time: 10 minutes / Cook time: 10 minutes

Ingredients:
- 300g green beans, trimmed
- 30g grated Parmesan cheese
- 2 cloves garlic, minced
- 15ml olive oil
- Salt and black pepper, to taste

Preparation instructions:
1. Preheat the Air Fryer to 200°C for 5 minutes.
2. In a bowl, toss green beans with grated Parmesan cheese, minced garlic, olive oil, salt, and black pepper until well coated.
3. Place the seasoned green beans in the Air Fryer basket.

4. Air fry for 10 minutes or until the green beans are tender and slightly crispy, shaking the basket occasionally.
5. Serve the Parmesan and Garlic Air-Fried Green Beans hot as a tasty side dish.

Panko-Crusted Air-Fried Mushrooms with Aioli

Serves: 4 / Prep time: 15 minutes / Cook time: 12 minutes

Ingredients:
- 200g button mushrooms, cleaned and halved
- 60g plain flour
- 1 egg, beaten
- 75g panko breadcrumbs
- 1/2 tsp smoked paprika
- Salt and black pepper, to taste
- Vegetable oil spray
- 60ml mayonnaise
- 1 clove garlic, minced
- 1/2 lemon, juiced

Preparation instructions:
1. Preheat the Air Fryer to 200°C for 5 minutes.
2. In separate bowls, place flour, beaten egg, and a mixture of panko breadcrumbs, smoked paprika, salt, and black pepper.
3. Dip mushroom halves first in flour, then in egg, and finally in the breadcrumb mixture, pressing gently to adhere.
4. Place the breaded mushrooms in the Air Fryer basket. Lightly spray with vegetable oil.
5. Air fry for 12 minutes or until the mushrooms are golden and crispy, turning halfway through.
6. In a small bowl, mix mayonnaise, minced garlic, and lemon juice to make the aioli dipping sauce.
7. Serve the Panko-Crusted Air-Fried Mushrooms hot, with aioli sauce on the side for dipping.

Spicy Sweet Potato Fries with Chipotle Dip

Serves: 4 / Prep time: 15 minutes / Cook time: 20 minutes

Ingredients:
- 2 large sweet potatoes, peeled and cut into fries
- 30ml olive oil
- 1 tsp smoked paprika
- 1/2 tsp ground cumin
- 1/2 tsp chilli powder
- Salt and black pepper, to taste
- Chipotle Dip:
- 60ml mayonnaise
- 1/2 lime, juiced
- 1-2 tsp adobo sauce from canned chipotle peppers
- Salt and black pepper, to taste

Preparation instructions:
1. Preheat the Air Fryer to 200°C for 5 minutes.
2. In a bowl, toss sweet potato fries with olive oil, smoked paprika, ground cumin, chilli powder, salt, and black pepper until well coated.
3. Arrange the seasoned sweet potato fries in the Air Fryer basket.
4. Air fry for 20 minutes or until the fries are crispy and golden, shaking the basket occasionally.
5. In a small bowl, mix mayonnaise, adobo sauce, lime juice, salt, and black pepper to make the chipotle dip.
6. Serve the Spicy Sweet Potato Fries hot, with chipotle dip on the side for dipping.

Air-Fried Halloumi and Tomato Skewers

Serves: 4 / Prep time: 15 minutes / Cook time: 10 minutes

Ingredients:
- 250g halloumi cheese, cut into cubes
- 16 cherry tomatoes
- 30ml olive oil
- 1 tsp dried oregano
- Salt and black pepper, to taste
- Fresh basil leaves, for garnish

Preparation instructions:
1. Preheat the Air Fryer to 200°C for 5 minutes.
2. In a bowl, combine halloumi cubes, cherry tomatoes, olive oil, dried oregano, salt, and black pepper. Toss gently to coat.
3. Thread halloumi cubes and cherry tomatoes alternately onto skewers.
4. Place the skewers in the Air Fryer basket.
5. Air fry for 10 minutes, turning occasionally, or until the halloumi is golden and crispy.
6. Remove from the Air Fryer and garnish with fresh basil leaves. Serve hot.

Crispy Air-Fried Onion Rings with Tangy Dip

Serves: 4 / Prep time: 15 minutes / Cook time: 10 minutes

Ingredients:
- 2 large onions, sliced into rings
- 100g plain flour
- 2 eggs, beaten
- 75g breadcrumbs
- 1 tsp smoked paprika
- 1/2 tsp garlic powder
- Salt and black pepper, to taste
- Vegetable oil spray
- Tangy Dip:
- 150ml Greek yoghurt
- 1 tbsp lemon juice
- 1 tbsp fresh parsley, chopped
- Salt and black pepper, to taste

Preparation instructions:
1. Preheat the Air Fryer to 200°C for 5 minutes.
2. In separate bowls, place flour, beaten eggs, and a mixture of breadcrumbs, smoked paprika, garlic powder, salt, and black pepper.
3. Dip onion rings first in flour, then in egg, and finally in the breadcrumb mixture, pressing gently to adhere.
4. Arrange the coated onion rings in the Air Fryer basket. Lightly spray with vegetable oil.
5. Air fry for 10 minutes or until the onion rings are golden and crispy, turning halfway through.
6. In a small bowl, mix Greek yoghurt, lemon juice, fresh parsley, salt, and black pepper to make the tangy dip.
7. Serve the Crispy Air-Fried Onion Rings hot, with tangy dip on the side for dipping.

Air-Fried Cornbread Muffins with Honey Butter

Serves: 4 / Prep time: 10 minutes / Cook time: 15 minutes

Ingredients:
- 200g cornmeal
- 100g plain flour
- 2 tsp baking powder
- 1/2 tsp baking soda
- 1/2 tsp salt
- 240 ml buttermilk
- 2 eggs
- 60g unsalted butter, melted
- Honey Butter:
- 60g unsalted butter, softened
- 2 tbsp honey
- Pinch of salt

Preparation instructions:
1. Preheat the Air Fryer to 180°C for 5 minutes.
2. In a bowl, combine cornmeal, plain flour, baking powder, baking soda, and salt.
3. In another bowl, whisk buttermilk, eggs, and melted butter.
4. Pour the wet ingredients into the dry ingredients and stir until just combined.
5. Divide the batter evenly among 8 muffin cups lined with paper liners.
6. Place the muffin cups in the Air Fryer basket.
7. Air fry for 15 minutes or until a toothpick inserted into the muffins comes out clean.
8. In a small bowl, mix softened butter, honey, and a pinch of salt to make the honey butter.
9. Serve the Air-Fried Cornbread Muffins hot, with a dollop of honey butter on top.

Air-Fried Jalapeño Poppers with Creamy Ranch

Serves: 4 / Prep time: 20 minutes / Cook time: 12 minutes

Ingredients:
- 8 large jalapeño peppers, halved and seeded
- 100g cream cheese, softened
- 50g shredded cheddar cheese
- 2 green onions, finely chopped
- 50g plain flour
- 2 eggs, beaten
- 75g breadcrumbs
- 1/2 tsp smoked paprika
- 1/2 tsp garlic powder
- Salt and black pepper, to taste
- Creamy Ranch Dip:
- 150ml sour cream
- 1 tbsp fresh dill, chopped
- 1 tbsp fresh parsley, chopped
- 1 clove garlic, minced
- 1/2 lemon, juiced
- Salt and black pepper, to taste

Preparation instructions:
1. Preheat the Air Fryer to 200°C for 5 minutes.
2. In a bowl, combine cream cheese, shredded cheddar cheese, and chopped green onions. Mix well.
3. Stuff each jalapeño half with the cream cheese mixture.

4. In separate bowls, place flour, beaten eggs, and a mixture of breadcrumbs, smoked paprika, garlic powder, salt, and black pepper.
5. Dip each stuffed jalapeño first in flour, then in egg, and finally in the breadcrumb mixture, pressing gently to adhere.
6. Arrange the coated jalapeño poppers in the Air Fryer basket.
7. Air fry for 12 minutes or until the poppers are golden and crispy, turning halfway through.
8. In a small bowl, mix sour cream, fresh dill, fresh parsley, minced garlic, lemon juice, salt, and black pepper to make the creamy ranch dip.
9. Serve the Air-Fried Jalapeño Poppers hot, with creamy ranch dip on the side for dipping.

Crispy Air-Fried Polenta Fries with Marinara

Serves: 4 / Prep time: 15 minutes / Cook time: 15 minutes

Ingredients:
- 400g polenta, cooked and cooled, cut into fries
- 50g grated Parmesan cheese
- 1/2 tsp dried oregano
- 1/2 tsp garlic powder
- 1/2 tsp onion powder
- Salt and black pepper, to taste
- Vegetable oil spray
- Marinara Dip:
- 200g tomato passata
- 1 clove garlic, minced
- 1/2 tsp dried basil
- 1/2 tsp dried oregano
- Salt and black pepper, to taste

Preparation instructions:
1. Preheat the Air Fryer to 200°C for 5 minutes.
2. In a bowl, combine cooked polenta fries, grated Parmesan cheese, dried oregano, garlic powder, onion powder, salt, and black pepper. Toss gently to coat.
3. Lightly spray the polenta fries with vegetable oil.
4. Arrange the coated polenta fries in the Air Fryer basket.
5. Air fry for 15 minutes or until the fries are crispy and golden, shaking the basket occasionally.
6. In a small saucepan, combine tomato passata, minced garlic, dried basil, dried oregano, salt, and black pepper. Simmer over low heat for 5 minutes, stirring occasionally.
7. Serve the Crispy Air-Fried Polenta Fries hot, with marinara dip on the side for dipping.

Stuffed Mini Peppers with Cream Cheese and Herbs

Serves: 4 / Prep time: 15 minutes / Cook time: 10 minutes

Ingredients:
- 200g mini sweet peppers, halved and seeded
- 150g cream cheese, softened
- 2 tbsp fresh chives, chopped
- 2 tbsp fresh parsley, chopped
- Salt and black pepper, to taste
- 30g grated Parmesan cheese

Preparation instructions:
1. Preheat the Air Fryer to 180°C for 5 minutes.
2. In a bowl, mix softened cream cheese, fresh chives, fresh parsley, salt, and black pepper.
3. Fill each mini pepper half with the cream cheese mixture.
4. Sprinkle grated Parmesan cheese over the stuffed peppers.
5. Place the stuffed mini peppers in the Air Fryer basket.
6. Air fry for 10 minutes or until the peppers are tender and the cheese is melted and lightly browned.
7. Remove from the Air Fryer and let cool for a few minutes before serving.

Air-Fried Pesto Potato Wedges

Serves: 4 / Prep time: 15 minutes / Cook time: 20 minutes

Ingredients:
- 600g potatoes, cut into wedges
- 30ml olive oil
- 2 tbsp pesto sauce
- Salt and black pepper, to taste
- Fresh basil leaves, for garnish

Preparation instructions:
1. Preheat the Air Fryer to 200°C for 5 minutes.
2. In a bowl, combine potato wedges, olive oil, pesto sauce, salt, and black pepper. Toss

gently to coat.
3. Place the seasoned potato wedges in the Air Fryer basket.
4. Air fry for 20 minutes or until the potato wedges are crispy and golden, shaking the basket occasionally for even cooking.
5. Remove from the Air Fryer and garnish with fresh basil leaves. Serve hot.

Air-Fried Pickle Spears with Dill Dip

Serves: 4 / Prep time: 15 minutes / Cook time: 10 minutes

Ingredients:
- 200g dill pickle spears
- 100g plain flour
- 2 eggs, beaten
- 75g breadcrumbs
- 1/2 tsp garlic powder
- 1/2 tsp paprika
- Salt and black pepper, to taste
- Dill Dip:
- 150ml sour cream
- 1 tbsp fresh dill, chopped
- 1 clove garlic, minced
- 1/2 lemon, juiced
- Salt and black pepper, to taste

Preparation instructions:
1. Preheat the Air Fryer to 200°C for 5 minutes.
2. In separate bowls, place flour, beaten eggs, and a mixture of breadcrumbs, garlic powder, paprika, salt, and black pepper.
3. Dip each pickle spear first in flour, then in egg, and finally in the breadcrumb mixture, pressing gently to adhere.
4. Arrange the coated pickle spears in the Air Fryer basket.
5. Air fry for 10 minutes or until the pickle spears are crispy and golden, turning halfway through.
6. In a small bowl, mix sour cream, fresh dill, minced garlic, lemon juice, salt, and black pepper to make the dill dip.
7. Serve the Air-Fried Pickle Spears hot, with dill dip on the side for dipping.

Crispy Air-Fried Avocado Fries with Lime Dip

Serves: 4 / Prep time: 15 minutes / Cook time: 12 minutes

Ingredients:
- 2 avocados, sliced into fries
- 100g plain flour
- 2 eggs, beaten
- 75g breadcrumbs
- 1/2 tsp smoked paprika
- 1/2 tsp garlic powder
- Salt and black pepper, to taste
- Lime Dip:
- 150ml Greek yoghurt
- Zest and juice of 1 lime
- 1 tbsp fresh coriander, chopped
- Salt and black pepper, to taste

Preparation instructions:
1. Preheat the Air Fryer to 200°C for 5 minutes.
2. In separate bowls, place flour, beaten eggs, and a mixture of breadcrumbs, smoked paprika, garlic powder, salt, and black pepper.
3. Dip each avocado fry first in flour, then in egg, and finally in the breadcrumb mixture, pressing gently to adhere.
4. Arrange the coated avocado fries in the Air Fryer basket.
5. Air fry for 12 minutes or until the avocado fries are crispy and golden, turning halfway through.
6. In a small bowl, mix Greek yoghurt, lime zest, lime juice, fresh coriander, salt, and black pepper to make the lime dip.
7. Serve the Crispy Air-Fried Avocado Fries hot, with lime dip on the side for dipping.

Air-Fried Stuffed Jalapeños with Bacon and Cheese

Serves: 4 / Prep time: 20 minutes / Cook time: 10 minutes

Ingredients:
- 8 large jalapeños, halved and seeded
- 100g cream cheese, softened
- 50g cheddar cheese, shredded

- 8 slices bacon, cooked and crumbled
- 1/2 tsp smoked paprika
- 1/2 tsp onion powder
- Salt and black pepper, to taste

Preparation instructions:
1. Preheat the Air Fryer to 180°C for 5 minutes.
2. In a bowl, mix softened cream cheese, cheddar cheese, cooked bacon, smoked paprika, onion powder, salt, and black pepper.
3. Fill each jalapeño half with the cream cheese mixture.
4. Place the stuffed jalapeños in the Air Fryer basket.
5. Air fry for 10 minutes or until the jalapeños are tender and the cheese is melted and lightly browned.
6. Remove from the Air Fryer and let cool for a few minutes before serving.

Garlic Herb Air-Fried Breaded Mushrooms

Serves: 4 / Prep time: 15 minutes / Cook time: 10 minutes

Ingredients:
- 200g button mushrooms, cleaned and halved
- 100g plain flour
- 2 eggs, beaten
- 75g breadcrumbs
- 1/2 tsp garlic powder
- 1/2 tsp dried mixed herbs
- Salt and black pepper, to taste

Preparation instructions:
1. Preheat the Air Fryer to 200°C for 5 minutes.
2. In separate bowls, place flour, beaten eggs, and a mixture of breadcrumbs, garlic powder, dried mixed herbs, salt, and black pepper.
3. Dip each mushroom half first in flour, then in egg, and finally in the breadcrumb mixture, pressing gently to adhere.
4. Arrange the coated mushrooms in the Air Fryer basket.
5. Air fry for 10 minutes or until the mushrooms are golden and crispy, turning halfway through.
6. Remove from the Air Fryer and let cool for a few minutes before serving.

Air-Fried Halloumi Fritters with Sweet Chilli Sauce

Serves: 4 / Prep time: 20 minutes / Cook time: 10 minutes

Ingredients:
- 250g halloumi cheese, grated
- 50g plain flour
- 2 eggs, beaten
- 75g breadcrumbs
- 1/2 tsp smoked paprika
- 1/2 tsp dried oregano
- Salt and black pepper, to taste
- Sweet Chilli Sauce:
- 150ml sweet chilli sauce
- 1 tbsp soy sauce
- 1 clove garlic, minced
- 1/2 lime, juiced

Preparation instructions:
1. Preheat the Air Fryer to 200°C for 5 minutes.
2. In a bowl, combine grated halloumi cheese, plain flour, smoked paprika, dried oregano, salt, and black pepper.
3. Shape the mixture into small fritters.
4. Dip each fritter first in flour, then in egg, and finally in the breadcrumb mixture, pressing gently to adhere.
5. Arrange the coated halloumi fritters in the Air Fryer basket.
6. Air fry for 10 minutes or until the fritters are golden and crispy, turning halfway through.
7. In a small bowl, mix sweet chilli sauce, soy sauce, minced garlic, and lime juice to prepare the dipping sauce.
8. Serve the Air-Fried Halloumi Fritters hot, with sweet chilli sauce on the side for dipping.

Crispy Air-Fried Artichoke Hearts with Lemon Aioli

Serves: 4 / Prep time: 20 minutes / Cook time: 12 minutes

Ingredients:
- 200g canned artichoke hearts, drained and halved
- 100g plain flour
- 2 eggs, beaten
- 75g breadcrumbs

- 1/2 tsp garlic powder
- 1/2 tsp dried parsley
  - Salt and black pepper, to taste
- Lemon Aioli:
- 150ml mayonnaise
- 1 clove garlic, minced
- Zest and juice of 1/2 lemon
- Salt and black pepper, to taste

Preparation instructions:
1. Preheat the Air Fryer to 200°C for 5 minutes.
2. In separate bowls, place flour, beaten eggs, and a mixture of breadcrumbs, garlic powder, dried parsley, salt, and black pepper.
3. Dip each artichoke heart first in flour, then in egg, and finally in the breadcrumb mixture, pressing gently to adhere.
4. Arrange the coated artichoke hearts in the Air Fryer basket.
5. Air fry for 12 minutes or until the artichoke hearts are crispy and golden, turning halfway through.
6. In a small bowl, mix mayonnaise, minced garlic, lemon zest, lemon juice, salt, and black pepper to make the lemon aioli.
7. Serve the Crispy Air-Fried Artichoke Hearts hot, with lemon aioli on the side for dipping.

Air-Fried Sweet Corn Fritters with Yoghurt Dip

Serves: 4 / Prep time: 15 minutes / Cook time: 10 minutes

Ingredients:
- 200g sweet corn kernels (fresh or canned), drained
- 100g plain flour
- 2 eggs, beaten
- 1/2 red onion, finely chopped
- 1/2 red chilli, finely chopped
- 1/2 tsp ground cumin
- 1/2 tsp baking powder
- Salt and black pepper, to taste
- Yoghurt Dip:
- 150ml Greek yoghurt
- 1 tbsp fresh coriander, chopped
- 1/2 lime, juiced
- Salt and black pepper, to taste

Preparation instructions:
1. Preheat the Air Fryer to 200°C for 5 minutes.
2. In a bowl, combine sweet corn kernels, plain flour, beaten eggs, finely chopped red onion, finely chopped red chilli, ground cumin, baking powder, salt, and black pepper.
3. Mix until well combined to form a thick batter.
4. Drop spoonfuls of the batter into the Air Fryer basket, forming fritters.
5. Air fry for 10 minutes or until the sweet corn fritters are golden and crispy, turning halfway through.
6. In a small bowl, mix Greek yoghurt, fresh coriander, lime juice, salt, and black pepper to prepare the yoghurt dip.
7. Serve the Air-Fried Sweet Corn Fritters hot, with yoghurt dip on the side for dipping.

Crispy Air-Fried Asparagus Spears with Lemon Zest

Serves: 4 / Prep time: 10 minutes / Cook time: 10 minutes

Ingredients:
- 200g asparagus spears, trimmed
- 100g plain flour
- 2 eggs, beaten
- 75g breadcrumbs
- Zest of 1 lemon
- 1/2 tsp dried thyme
- Salt and black pepper, to taste

Preparation instructions:
1. Preheat the Air Fryer to 200°C for 5 minutes.
2. In separate bowls, place flour, beaten eggs, and a mixture of breadcrumbs, lemon zest, dried thyme, salt, and black pepper.
3. Dip each asparagus spear first in flour, then in egg, and finally in the breadcrumb mixture, pressing gently to adhere.
4. Arrange the coated asparagus spears in the Air Fryer basket.
5. Air fry for 10 minutes or until the asparagus spears are crispy and golden, turning halfway through.
6. Remove from the Air Fryer and let cool for a few minutes before serving.

Chapter 7: Hearty Stew Recipes

Air-Fried Hearty Beef and Ale Stew

Serves: 4 / Prep time: 15 minutes / Cook time: 1 hour 30 minutes

Ingredients:
- 500g stewing beef, cubed
- 60g plain flour
- 2 tbsp vegetable oil
- 2 onions, chopped
- 2 carrots, peeled and sliced
- 2 parsnips, peeled and sliced
- 2 cloves garlic, minced
- 500ml beef stock
- 330ml ale (such as Guinness)
- 2 tbsp tomato paste
- 1 bay leaf
- Salt and black pepper, to taste
- Fresh parsley, chopped (for garnish)

Preparation instructions:
1. Toss the cubed beef in plain flour until coated evenly.
2. Preheat the Air Fryer to 180°C (360°F).
3. Heat vegetable oil in the Air Fryer basket. Add the coated beef cubes and cook until browned on all sides. Remove and set aside.
4. In the same basket, add the chopped onions, carrots, parsnips, and minced garlic. Air fry for 5-7 minutes until the vegetables are softened.
5. Return the browned beef to the basket. Add beef stock, ale, tomato paste, bay leaf, salt, and black pepper.
6. Cook in the Air Fryer at 160°C (320°F) for 1 hour 30 minutes, stirring occasionally, until the beef is tender and flavours meld together.
7. Garnish with chopped fresh parsley before serving.

Air-Fried Traditional Lamb and Vegetable Stew

Serves: 4 / Prep time: 15 minutes / Cook time: 1 hour 30 minutes

Ingredients:
- 500g lamb stew meat, cubed
- 60g plain flour
- 2 tbsp vegetable oil
- 2 onions, chopped
- 3 carrots, peeled and sliced
- 2 potatoes, peeled and cubed
- 2 cloves garlic, minced
- 500ml lamb or vegetable stock
- 1 tbsp tomato paste
- 1 tsp dried rosemary
- Salt and black pepper, to taste
- Fresh mint, chopped (for garnish)

Preparation instructions:
1. Toss the lamb cubes in plain flour until coated evenly.
2. Preheat the Air Fryer to 180°C (360°F).
3. Heat vegetable oil in the Air Fryer basket. Add the coated lamb cubes and cook until browned on all sides. Remove and set aside.
4. In the same basket, add the chopped onions, carrots, potatoes, and minced garlic. Air fry for 5-7 minutes until the vegetables are softened.
5. Return the browned lamb to the basket. Add lamb or vegetable stock, tomato paste, dried rosemary, salt, and black pepper.
6. Cook in the Air Fryer at 160°C (320°F) for 1 hour 30 minutes, stirring occasionally, until the lamb is tender and flavours meld together.
7. Garnish with chopped fresh mint before serving.

Air-Fried Rich Guinness Beef Stew

Serves: 4 / Prep time: 15 minutes / Cook time: 1 hour 30 minutes

Ingredients:
- 500g stewing beef, cubed
- 60g plain flour
- 2 tbsp vegetable oil
- 2 onions, chopped

- 3 carrots, peeled and sliced
- 2 potatoes, peeled and cubed
- 2 cloves garlic, minced
- 500ml beef stock
- 330ml Guinness stout
- 2 tbsp tomato paste
- 1 bay leaf
- Salt and black pepper, to taste
- Fresh parsley, chopped (for garnish)

Preparation instructions:
1. Toss the beef cubes in plain flour until coated evenly.
2. Preheat the Air Fryer to 180°C (360°F).
3. Heat vegetable oil in the Air Fryer basket. Add the coated beef cubes and cook until browned on all sides. Remove and set aside.
4. In the same basket, add the chopped onions, carrots, potatoes, and minced garlic. Air fry for 5-7 minutes until the vegetables are softened.
5. Return the browned beef to the basket. Add beef stock, Guinness stout, tomato paste, bay leaf, salt, and black pepper.
6. Cook in the Air Fryer at 160°C (320°F) for 1 hour 30 minutes, stirring occasionally, until the beef is tender and flavours meld together.
7. Garnish with chopped fresh parsley before serving.

Air-Fried Classic Chicken and Mushroom Stew

Serves: 4 / Prep time: 15 minutes / Cook time: 1 hour 15 minutes

Ingredients:
- 4 chicken thighs, bone-in and skin-on
- 60g plain flour
- 2 tbsp vegetable oil
- 2 onions, chopped
- 250g mushrooms, sliced
- 2 cloves garlic, minced
- 500ml chicken stock
- 1 tbsp tomato paste
- 1 tsp dried thyme
- Salt and black pepper, to taste
- Fresh parsley, chopped (for garnish)

Preparation instructions:
1. Toss the chicken thighs in plain flour until coated evenly.
2. Preheat the Air Fryer to 180°C (360°F).
3. Heat vegetable oil in the Air Fryer basket. Add the coated chicken thighs and cook until browned on all sides. Remove and set aside.
4. In the same basket, add the chopped onions, mushrooms, and minced garlic. Air fry for 5-7 minutes until the vegetables are softened.
5. Return the browned chicken thighs to the basket. Add chicken stock, tomato paste, dried thyme, salt, and black pepper.
6. Cook in the Air Fryer at 160°C (320°F) for 1 hour 15 minutes, stirring occasionally, until the chicken is cooked through and flavours meld together.
7. Garnish with chopped fresh parsley before serving.

Air-Fried Homely Vegetable and Barley Stew

Serves: 4 / Prep time: 15 minutes / Cook time: 1 hour 15 minutes

Ingredients:
- 100g pearl barley, rinsed
- 2 tbsp vegetable oil
- 2 onions, chopped
- 3 carrots, peeled and sliced
- 2 potatoes, peeled and cubed
- 2 parsnips, peeled and sliced
- 2 cloves garlic, minced
- 1.5 litres vegetable stock
- 1 tbsp tomato paste
- 1 tsp dried thyme
- Salt and black pepper, to taste
- Fresh parsley, chopped (for garnish)

Preparation instructions:
1. Preheat the Air Fryer to 180°C (360°F).
2. Heat vegetable oil in the Air Fryer basket. Add the chopped onions, carrots, potatoes, parsnips, and minced garlic. Air fry for 5-7 minutes until the vegetables are slightly softened.
3. Add rinsed pearl barley, vegetable stock,

tomato paste, dried thyme, salt, and black pepper to the basket.
4. Cook in the Air Fryer at 160°C (320°F) for 1 hour 15 minutes, stirring occasionally, until the barley and vegetables are tender and flavours meld together.
5. Garnish with chopped fresh parsley before serving.

Smoky Sausage and Bean Stew

Serves: 4 / Prep time: 15 minutes / Cook time: 25 minutes

Ingredients:
- 8 cooked sausages, sliced
- 400g canned cannellini beans, drained and rinsed
- 1 onion, chopped
- 2 cloves garlic, minced
- 400g canned chopped tomatoes
- 500ml beef or vegetable stock
- 1 tsp smoked paprika
- 1/2 tsp cumin powder
- Salt and black pepper, to taste
- Fresh parsley, chopped (for garnish)

Preparation instructions:
1. Preheat the Air Fryer to 180°C for 5 minutes.
2. In a large bowl, combine sliced sausages, cannellini beans, chopped onion, minced garlic, chopped tomatoes, stock, smoked paprika, cumin powder, salt, and black pepper.
3. Divide the mixture between 2 silicone muffin cups in each basket of the Air Fryer.
4. Air fry at 180°C for 25 minutes or until the stew is hot and bubbling.
5. Garnish with chopped fresh parsley before serving.

Rustic Pork and Cider Stew

Serves: 4 / Prep time: 15 minutes / Cook time: 25 minutes

Ingredients:
- 500g pork shoulder, cubed
- 1 onion, chopped
- 2 carrots, peeled and sliced
- 2 parsnips, peeled and sliced
- 2 cloves garlic, minced
- 500ml dry cider
- 500ml chicken stock
- 2 tbsp tomato paste
- 1 tsp dried thyme
- Salt and black pepper, to taste
- Fresh parsley, chopped (for garnish)

Preparation instructions:
1. Preheat the Air Fryer to 180°C for 5 minutes.
2. In a large bowl, combine cubed pork, chopped onion, sliced carrots, sliced parsnips, minced garlic, cider, chicken stock, tomato paste, dried thyme, salt, and black pepper.
3. Divide the mixture between 2 silicone muffin cups in each basket of the Air Fryer.
4. Air fry at 180°C for 25 minutes or until the stew is hot and the pork is cooked through.
5. Garnish with chopped fresh parsley before serving.

Fragrant Thai Green Curry Stew

Serves: 4 / Prep time: 15 minutes / Cook time: 25 minutes

Ingredients:
- 400g chicken breast, sliced
- 200ml coconut milk
- 200ml chicken stock
- 2 tbsp Thai green curry paste
- 1 onion, sliced
- 1 red pepper, sliced
- 1 courgette, sliced
- 1 tbsp fish sauce
- 1 tsp brown sugar
- Fresh coriander, chopped (for garnish)
- Cooked jasmine rice (for serving)

Preparation instructions:
1. Preheat the Air Fryer to 180°C for 5 minutes.
2. In a large bowl, combine sliced chicken, coconut milk, chicken stock, green curry paste, sliced onion, sliced red pepper, sliced courgette, fish sauce, and brown sugar.

3. Divide the mixture between 2 silicone muffin cups in each basket of the Air Fryer.
4. Air fry at 180°C for 25 minutes or until the chicken is cooked through and the vegetables are tender.
5. Garnish with chopped fresh coriander and serve with cooked jasmine rice.

Hearty Lentil and Vegetable Stew

Serves: 4 / Prep time: 15 minutes / Cook time: 25 minutes

Ingredients:
- 200g dried green lentils, rinsed
- 1 onion, chopped
- 2 carrots, peeled and sliced
- 2 potatoes, peeled and cubed
- 2 cloves garlic, minced
- 1.5 litres vegetable stock
- 1 tsp ground cumin
- 1/2 tsp smoked paprika
- Salt and black pepper, to taste
- Fresh parsley, chopped (for garnish)

Preparation instructions:
1. Preheat the Air Fryer to 180°C for 5 minutes.
2. In a large bowl, combine rinsed lentils, chopped onion, sliced carrots, cubed potatoes, minced garlic, vegetable stock, ground cumin, smoked paprika, salt, and black pepper.
3. Divide the mixture between 2 silicone muffin cups in each basket of the Air Fryer.
4. Air fry at 180°C for 25 minutes or until the lentils and vegetables are tender.
5. Garnish with chopped fresh parsley before serving.

Spicy Chickpea and Spinach Stew

Serves: 4 / Prep time: 15 minutes / Cook time: 25 minutes

Ingredients:
- 2 cans (400g each) chickpeas, drained and rinsed
- 1 onion, chopped
- 2 cloves garlic, minced
- 400g canned chopped tomatoes
- 200ml vegetable stock
- 2 tsp ground cumin
- 1/2 tsp cayenne pepper
- 200g fresh spinach
- Salt and black pepper, to taste
- Fresh coriander, chopped (for garnish)
- Cooked couscous (for serving)

Preparation instructions:
1. Preheat the Air Fryer to 180°C for 5 minutes.
2. In a large bowl, combine chickpeas, chopped onion, minced garlic, chopped tomatoes, vegetable stock, ground cumin, cayenne pepper, fresh spinach, salt, and black pepper.
3. Divide the mixture between 2 silicone muffin cups in each basket of the Air Fryer.
4. Air fry at 180°C for 25 minutes or until the stew is hot and bubbling, and the spinach is wilted.
5. Garnish with chopped fresh coriander and serve with cooked couscous.

Creamy Seafood Chowder

Serves: 4 / Prep time: 15 minutes / Cook time: 25 minutes

Ingredients:
- 300g mixed seafood (such as prawns, fish, and scallops), chopped
- 1 onion, finely chopped
- 2 cloves garlic, minced
- 2 potatoes, peeled and diced
- 500ml fish stock
- 200ml double cream
- 60ml white wine
- 1 bay leaf
- Salt and black pepper, to taste
- Fresh parsley, chopped (for garnish)

Preparation instructions:
1. Preheat the Air Fryer to 180°C for 5 minutes.
2. In a large bowl, combine mixed seafood, finely chopped onion, minced garlic, diced potatoes, fish stock, double cream, white wine, bay leaf, salt, and black pepper.

3. Divide the mixture between 2 silicone muffin cups in each basket of the Air Fryer.
4. Air fry at 180°C for 25 minutes or until the potatoes are tender and the seafood is cooked through.
5. Garnish with chopped fresh parsley before serving.

Moroccan-inspired Lamb and Apricot Stew

Serves: 4 / Prep time: 15 minutes / Cook time: 25 minutes

Ingredients:
- 500g lamb shoulder, diced
- 1 onion, chopped
- 2 carrots, peeled and sliced
- 2 cloves garlic, minced
- 200g dried apricots, halved
- 500ml lamb stock
- 1 tsp ground cumin
- 1 tsp ground coriander
- 1/2 tsp ground cinnamon
- Salt and black pepper, to taste
- Fresh coriander, chopped (for garnish)

Preparation instructions:
1. Preheat the Air Fryer to 180°C for 5 minutes.
2. In a large bowl, combine diced lamb, chopped onion, sliced carrots, minced garlic, halved apricots, lamb stock, ground cumin, ground coriander, ground cinnamon, salt, and black pepper.
3. Divide the mixture between 2 silicone muffin cups in each basket of the Air Fryer.
4. Air fry at 180°C for 25 minutes or until the lamb is tender and the flavours are well melded.
5. Garnish with chopped fresh coriander before serving.

Savoury Venison and Red Wine Stew

Serves: 4 / Prep time: 15 minutes / Cook time: 25 minutes

Ingredients:
- 500g venison, diced
- 1 onion, chopped
- 2 carrots, peeled and sliced
- 2 cloves garlic, minced
- 500ml red wine
- 500ml venison or beef stock
- 2 tbsp tomato paste
- 1 tsp dried thyme
- Salt and black pepper, to taste
- Fresh parsley, chopped (for garnish)

Preparation instructions:
1. Preheat the Air Fryer to 180°C for 5 minutes.
2. In a large bowl, combine diced venison, chopped onion, sliced carrots, minced garlic, red wine, venison or beef stock, tomato paste, dried thyme, salt, and black pepper.
3. Divide the mixture between 2 silicone muffin cups in each basket of the Air Fryer.
4. Air fry at 180°C for 25 minutes or until the venison is tender and the stew is rich and flavorful.
5. Garnish with chopped fresh parsley before serving.

Cosy Potato and Leek Soup

Serves: 4 / Prep time: 15 minutes / Cook time: 25 minutes

Ingredients:
- 4 potatoes, peeled and diced
- 2 leeks, sliced
- 1 onion, chopped
- 2 cloves garlic, minced
- 1 litre vegetable stock
- 200ml double cream
- 2 tbsp butter
- Salt and black pepper, to taste
- Fresh chives, chopped (for garnish)

Preparation instructions:
1. Preheat the Air Fryer to 180°C for 5 minutes.
2. In a large bowl, combine diced potatoes, sliced leeks, chopped onion, minced garlic, vegetable stock, double cream, butter, salt, and black pepper.
3. Divide the mixture between 2 silicone muffin cups in each basket of the Air Fryer.
4. Air fry at 180°C for 25 minutes or until the

potatoes are tender.
5. Garnish with chopped fresh chives before serving.

Irish Lamb and Guinness Stew

Serves: 4 / Prep time: 15 minutes / Cook time: 25 minutes

Ingredients:
- 500g lamb stew meat, diced
- 1 onion, chopped
- 2 carrots, peeled and sliced
- 2 cloves garlic, minced
- 500ml Guinness stout
- 500ml lamb or beef stock
- 2 tbsp tomato paste
- 1 tsp dried rosemary
- Salt and black pepper, to taste
- Fresh parsley, chopped (for garnish)

Preparation instructions:
1. Preheat the Air Fryer to 180°C for 5 minutes.
2. In a large bowl, combine diced lamb, chopped onion, sliced carrots, minced garlic, Guinness stout, lamb or beef stock, tomato paste, dried rosemary, salt, and black pepper.
3. Divide the mixture between 2 silicone muffin cups in each basket of the Air Fryer.
4. Air fry at 180°C for 25 minutes or until the lamb is tender and the stew is rich and flavorful.
5. Garnish with chopped fresh parsley before serving.

Tuscan-inspired Tomato and Bread Stew

Serves: 4 / Prep time: 15 minutes / Cook time: 25 minutes

Ingredients:
- 400g canned chopped tomatoes
- 200g stale bread, torn into chunks
- 1 onion, finely chopped
- 2 cloves garlic, minced
- 500ml vegetable stock
- 60ml olive oil
- 1 tsp dried basil
- 1 tsp dried oregano
- Salt and black pepper, to taste
- Fresh basil, chopped (for garnish)

Preparation instructions:
1. Preheat the Air Fryer to 180°C for 5 minutes.
2. In a large bowl, combine chopped tomatoes, torn bread chunks, finely chopped onion, minced garlic, vegetable stock, olive oil, dried basil, dried oregano, salt, and black pepper.
3. Divide the mixture between 2 silicone muffin cups in each basket of the Air Fryer.
4. Air fry at 180°C for 25 minutes or until the bread is soaked through and the stew is thickened.
5. Garnish with chopped fresh basil before serving.

Spiced Pumpkin and Lentil Stew

Serves: 4 / Prep time: 15 minutes / Cook time: 25 minutes

Ingredients:
- 400g pumpkin, peeled and diced
- 200g red lentils
- 1 onion, chopped
- 2 cloves garlic, minced
- 500ml vegetable stock
- 60ml coconut milk
- 1 tsp ground cumin
- 1/2 tsp ground turmeric
- Salt and black pepper, to taste
- Fresh coriander, chopped (for garnish)

Preparation instructions:
1. Preheat the Air Fryer to 180°C for 5 minutes.
2. In a large bowl, combine diced pumpkin, red lentils, chopped onion, minced garlic, vegetable stock, coconut milk, ground cumin, ground turmeric, salt, and black pepper.
3. Divide the mixture between 2 silicone muffin cups in each basket of the Air Fryer.
4. Air fry at 180°C for 25 minutes or until the pumpkin is tender and the lentils are cooked through.
5. Garnish with chopped fresh coriander before serving.

Spanish Chorizo and Chickpea Stew

Serves: 4 / Prep time: 15 minutes / Cook time: 25 minutes

Ingredients:
- 200g Spanish chorizo, sliced
- 400g canned chickpeas, drained and rinsed
- 1 onion, chopped
- 2 cloves garlic, minced
- 500ml chicken stock
- 1 tsp smoked paprika
- 1/2 tsp cayenne pepper
- Salt and black pepper, to taste
- Fresh parsley, chopped (for garnish)

Preparation instructions:
1. Preheat the Air Fryer to 180°C for 5 minutes.
2. In a large bowl, combine sliced chorizo, drained chickpeas, chopped onion, minced garlic, chicken stock, smoked paprika, cayenne pepper, salt, and black pepper.
3. Divide the mixture between 2 silicone muffin cups in each basket of the Air Fryer.
4. Air fry at 180°C for 25 minutes or until the chorizo is crispy and the stew is flavorful.
5. Garnish with chopped fresh parsley before serving.

Hearty Beef and Vegetable Casserole

Serves: 4 / Prep time: 15 minutes / Cook time: 25 minutes

Ingredients:
- 400g beef stew meat, diced
- 2 carrots, peeled and sliced
- 2 potatoes, peeled and diced
- 1 onion, chopped
- 500ml beef stock
- 2 tbsp tomato paste
- 1 tsp dried thyme
- Salt and black pepper, to taste
- Fresh thyme, chopped (for garnish)

Preparation instructions:
1. Preheat the Air Fryer to 180°C for 5 minutes.
2. In a large bowl, combine diced beef stew meat, sliced carrots, diced potatoes, chopped onion, beef stock, tomato paste, dried thyme, salt, and black pepper.
3. Divide the mixture between 2 silicone muffin cups in each basket of the Air Fryer.
4. Air fry at 180°C for 25 minutes or until the beef is tender and the vegetables are cooked through.
5. Garnish with chopped fresh thyme before serving.

Warm and Comforting Minestrone Stew

Serves: 4 / Prep time: 15 minutes / Cook time: 25 minutes

Ingredients:
- 400g canned mixed beans, drained and rinsed
- 200g pasta shells, cooked separately
- 1 onion, chopped
- 2 cloves garlic, minced
- 400g canned chopped tomatoes
- 500ml vegetable stock
- 1 tsp dried basil
- 1 tsp dried oregano
- Salt and black pepper, to taste
- Fresh parsley, chopped (for garnish)

Preparation instructions:
1. Preheat the Air Fryer to 180°C for 5 minutes.
2. In a large bowl, combine drained mixed beans, cooked pasta shells, chopped onion, minced garlic, chopped tomatoes, vegetable stock, dried basil, dried oregano, salt, and black pepper.
3. Divide the mixture between 2 silicone muffin cups in each basket of the Air Fryer.
4. Air fry at 180°C for 25 minutes or until the stew is hot and flavorful.
5. Garnish with chopped fresh parsley before serving.

Chapter 8: Fish and Seafood Recipes

Crispy Beer-Battered Fish and Chips

Serves: 4 / Prep time: 15 minutes / Cook time: 20 minutes

Ingredients:
- 400g white fish fillets (such as cod or haddock), cut into portions
- 150g all-purpose flour
- 200ml beer (lager or ale)
- 1/2 tsp baking powder
- Salt and black pepper, to taste
- 600g potatoes, peeled and cut into thick fries
- 30ml vegetable oil
- Lemon wedges, for serving
- Fresh parsley, chopped (for garnish)

Preparation instructions:
1. Preheat the Air Fryer to 200°C for 5 minutes.
2. In a bowl, whisk together the flour, beer, baking powder, salt, and black pepper to create a smooth batter.
3. Dip each fish fillet into the batter, ensuring it's well-coated, and place in the Air Fryer basket.
4. In another bowl, toss the potato fries with vegetable oil, salt, and black pepper.
5. Spread the fries in the second basket of the Air Fryer.
6. Air fry the fish at 200°C for 12-15 minutes or until golden and crispy, turning halfway through. Simultaneously, air fry the fries for 18-20 minutes until crispy, shaking the basket occasionally.
7. Serve the crispy fish and chips with lemon wedges, garnished with fresh chopped parsley.

Air-Fried Lemon Garlic Salmon Fillets

Serves: 4 / Prep time: 10 minutes / Cook time: 12 minutes

Ingredients:
- 4 salmon fillets
- Zest of 1 lemon
- 2 cloves garlic, minced
- 30ml olive oil
- Salt and black pepper, to taste
- Fresh dill, chopped (for garnish)

Preparation instructions:
1. Preheat the Air Fryer to 180°C for 5 minutes.
2. In a bowl, combine the lemon zest, minced garlic, olive oil, salt, and black pepper.
3. Brush the salmon fillets with the lemon garlic mixture, coating them evenly.
4. Place the salmon fillets in the Air Fryer basket.
5. Air fry at 180°C for 10-12 minutes or until the salmon is cooked through and flakes easily with a fork.
6. Garnish with chopped fresh dill before serving.

Spicy Cajun Shrimp Skewers

Serves: 4 / Prep time: 10 minutes / Cook time: 8 minutes

Ingredients:
- 400g large shrimp, peeled and deveined
- 30ml olive oil
- 1 tbsp Cajun seasoning
- 1/2 tsp paprika
- 1/2 tsp garlic powder
- Salt and black pepper, to taste
- Lemon wedges, for serving
- Fresh parsley, chopped (for garnish)

Preparation instructions:
1. Preheat the Air Fryer to 200°C for 5 minutes.
2. In a bowl, toss the shrimp with olive oil, Cajun seasoning, paprika, garlic powder, salt, and black pepper.
3. Thread the seasoned shrimp on skewers.
4. Place the shrimp skewers in the Air Fryer basket.
5. Air fry at 200°C for 6-8 minutes or until the shrimp are pink and cooked through, turning halfway through.
6. Serve the spicy Cajun shrimp skewers with lemon wedges, garnished with chopped fresh parsley.

Crispy Breaded Haddock Fillets

Serves: 4 / Prep time: 10 minutes / Cook time: 12 minutes

Ingredients:
- 4 haddock fillets
- 60g breadcrumbs
- 30g grated Parmesan cheese
- 1/2 tsp paprika
- 1/2 tsp garlic powder
- Salt and black pepper, to taste
- 1 egg, beaten
- Cooking spray
- Tartar sauce, for serving
- Fresh chives, chopped (for garnish)

Preparation instructions:
1. Preheat the Air Fryer to 200°C for 5 minutes.
2. In a bowl, combine breadcrumbs, grated Parmesan cheese, paprika, garlic powder, salt, and black pepper.
3. Dip each haddock fillet into the beaten egg, then coat with the breadcrumb mixture, pressing gently to adhere.
4. Spray the breaded fillets lightly with cooking spray.
5. Place the fillets in the Air Fryer basket.
6. Air fry at 200°C for 10-12 minutes or until the fillets are crispy and golden brown, turning halfway through.
7. Serve the crispy breaded haddock fillets with tartar sauce, garnished with chopped fresh chives.

Garlic Butter Prawns with Herbs

Serves: 4 / Prep time: 10 minutes / Cook time: 6 minutes

Ingredients:
- 400g large prawns, peeled and deveined
- 2 cloves garlic, minced
- 60g unsalted butter, melted
- 1 tbsp chopped fresh parsley
- Salt and black pepper, to taste
- Lemon wedges, for serving
- Fresh chives, chopped (for garnish)

Preparation instructions:
1. Preheat the Air Fryer to 200°C for 5 minutes.
2. In a bowl, toss the prawns with minced garlic, melted butter, chopped fresh parsley, salt, and black pepper.
3. Place the prawns in the Air Fryer basket.
4. Air fry at 200°C for 4-6 minutes or until the prawns are pink and cooked through, shaking the basket occasionally.
5. Serve the garlic butter prawns with lemon wedges, garnished with chopped fresh chives.

Air-Fried Fish Tacos with Lime Crema

Serves: 4 / Prep time: 15 minutes / Cook time: 10 minutes

Ingredients:
- 400g white fish fillets (such as cod or haddock)
- 100g all-purpose flour
- 2 eggs, beaten
- 100g breadcrumbs
- 1 tsp smoked paprika
- 1/2 tsp garlic powder
- Salt and black pepper, to taste
- 8 small corn tortillas
- 1 ripe avocado, sliced
- Fresh coriander, chopped (for garnish)
- Lime wedges, for serving
- For Lime Crema:
- 150ml sour cream
- Zest and juice of 1 lime
- Salt and black pepper, to taste

Preparation instructions:
1. Preheat the Air Fryer to 200°C for 5 minutes.
2. Cut the fish fillets into bite-sized pieces.
3. In three separate bowls, place flour, beaten eggs, and a mixture of breadcrumbs, smoked paprika, garlic powder, salt, and black pepper.
4. Dredge the fish pieces in flour, dip into the beaten eggs, then coat with the breadcrumb mixture.
5. Place the breaded fish pieces in the Air Fryer basket. Air fry at 200°C for 8-10 minutes

or until crispy and golden brown, turning halfway through.
6. While the fish is cooking, prepare the lime crema by mixing sour cream, lime zest, lime juice, salt, and black pepper in a bowl.
7. Warm the corn tortillas in the Air Fryer for 2 minutes.
8. Assemble the tacos: place a spoonful of lime crema on each tortilla, top with crispy fish pieces, avocado slices, and garnish with chopped coriander. Serve with lime wedges.

Sesame-Crusted Tuna Steaks

Serves: 4 / Prep time: 10 minutes / Cook time: 8 minutes

Ingredients:
- 4 tuna steaks
- 50g sesame seeds
- 2 tbsp soy sauce
- 1 tbsp honey
- 1 clove garlic, minced
- 1 tsp grated fresh ginger
- 1 tbsp sesame oil
- Fresh chives, chopped (for garnish)

Preparation instructions:
1. Preheat the Air Fryer to 200°C for 5 minutes.
2. Pat the tuna steaks dry with paper towels.
3. Coat each tuna steak with sesame seeds, pressing gently to adhere.
4. In a bowl, mix soy sauce, honey, minced garlic, grated ginger, and sesame oil to create a marinade.
5. Brush the marinade over the sesame-crusted tuna steaks.
6. Place the tuna steaks in the Air Fryer basket. Air fry at 200°C for 4 minutes per side or until the tuna is seared on the outside but still pink in the centre.
7. Garnish with chopped fresh chives before serving.

Air-Fried Coconut Shrimp with Mango Dipping Sauce

Serves: 4 / Prep time: 15 minutes / Cook time: 10 minutes

Ingredients:
- 400g large shrimp, peeled and deveined
- 100g desiccated coconut
- 50g all-purpose flour
- 2 eggs, beaten
- Salt and black pepper, to taste
- Cooking spray
- Lime wedges, for serving
- For Mango Dipping Sauce:
- 1 ripe mango, peeled and pitted
- 1 tbsp lime juice
- 1 tbsp honey
- 1/2 tsp red chilli flakes (optional)

Preparation instructions:
1. Preheat the Air Fryer to 200°C for 5 minutes.
2. In three separate bowls, place flour, beaten eggs, and desiccated coconut.
3. Season the shrimp with salt and black pepper.
4. Dredge the shrimp in flour, dip into the beaten eggs, then coat with desiccated coconut, pressing gently to adhere.
5. Place the coated shrimp in the Air Fryer basket, lightly spray with cooking spray. Air fry at 200°C for 8-10 minutes or until the shrimp are golden brown and crispy.
6. While the shrimp is cooking, prepare the mango dipping sauce by blending mango, lime juice, honey, and red chilli flakes (if using) until smooth.
7. Serve the air-fried coconut shrimp with mango dipping sauce and lime wedges.

Classic Fish Pie with a Twist

Serves: 4 / Prep time: 20 minutes / Cook time: 20 minutes

Ingredients:
- 400g mixed white fish fillets (such as cod, haddock, and salmon), cut into chunks
- 200ml whole milk
- 1 tbsp butter
- 2 tbsp all-purpose flour
- Salt and black pepper, to taste
- 300g potatoes, peeled and diced
- 200g broccoli florets
- 50g grated cheddar cheese

- For Topping:
- 300g sweet potatoes, peeled and diced
- 1 tbsp olive oil
- Salt and black pepper, to taste

Preparation instructions:
1. Preheat the Air Fryer to 180°C for 5 minutes.
2. In a saucepan, heat the milk until hot but not boiling.
3. In another saucepan, melt butter, add flour, and cook, stirring continuously, for 2 minutes to make a roux. Gradually whisk in the hot milk until the sauce thickens. Season with salt and black pepper.
4. Add the fish chunks to the sauce and stir gently. Set aside.
5. Steam the potatoes and broccoli until tender.
6. For the topping, toss sweet potatoes with olive oil, salt, and black pepper. Air fry at 180°C for 12-15 minutes or until crispy and golden brown.
7. Mix the steamed potatoes, broccoli, and fish in a baking dish. Sprinkle grated cheddar cheese on top.
8. Spread the air-fried sweet potato cubes over the fish mixture.
9. Air fry the fish pie at 180°C for 20 minutes or until the top is golden and the filling is bubbling.
10. Let it cool for a few minutes before serving.

Teriyaki Glazed Salmon with Sesame Seeds

Serves: 4 / Prep time: 10 minutes / Cook time: 12 minutes

Ingredients:
- 4 salmon fillets
- 4 tbsp teriyaki sauce
- 2 tbsp honey
- 1 tbsp soy sauce
- 1 clove garlic, minced
- 1 tsp grated fresh ginger
- 1 tbsp sesame seeds, toasted
- Fresh parsley, chopped (for garnish)

Preparation instructions:
1. Preheat the Air Fryer to 200°C for 5 minutes.
2. In a bowl, mix teriyaki sauce, honey, soy sauce, minced garlic, and grated ginger to make the glaze.
3. Brush the salmon fillets with the teriyaki glaze.
4. Place the salmon fillets in the Air Fryer basket. Air fry at 200°C for 12 minutes or until the salmon is cooked through and flakes easily with a fork, brushing with additional glaze halfway through the cooking time.
5. Sprinkle the air-fried salmon with toasted sesame seeds and chopped fresh parsley before serving.

Air-Fried Lemon Herb Scallops

Serves: 4 / Prep time: 10 minutes / Cook time: 8 minutes

Ingredients:
- 400g fresh scallops
- Zest and juice of 1 lemon
- 2 tbsp olive oil
- 2 cloves garlic, minced
- 1 tbsp fresh parsley, chopped
- Salt and black pepper, to taste
- Fresh chives, chopped (for garnish)

Preparation instructions:
1. Preheat the Air Fryer to 200°C for 5 minutes.
2. In a bowl, combine scallops, lemon zest, lemon juice, olive oil, minced garlic, fresh parsley, salt, and black pepper. Toss to coat the scallops evenly.
3. Place the marinated scallops in the Air Fryer basket. Air fry at 200°C for 8 minutes or until the scallops are cooked through and lightly golden brown, shaking the basket halfway through the cooking time.
4. Garnish with chopped fresh chives before serving.

Pesto Crusted Sea Bass Fillets

Serves: 4 / Prep time: 10 minutes / Cook time: 12 minutes

Ingredients:
- 4 sea bass fillets
- 4 tbsp pesto sauce

- 50g breadcrumbs
- 2 tbsp grated Parmesan cheese
- Salt and black pepper, to taste
- Fresh basil leaves (for garnish)

Preparation instructions:
1. Preheat the Air Fryer to 200°C for 5 minutes.
2. In a bowl, combine breadcrumbs, grated Parmesan cheese, salt, and black pepper.
3. Spread pesto sauce evenly over the sea bass fillets.
4. Coat the pesto-covered side of the fillets with the breadcrumb mixture, pressing gently to adhere.
5. Place the sea bass fillets in the Air Fryer basket, pesto side up. Air fry at 200°C for 12 minutes or until the fish is cooked through and the crust is golden brown and crispy.
6. Garnish with fresh basil leaves before serving.

Crispy Calamari Rings with Aioli Dip

Serves: 4 / Prep time: 15 minutes / Cook time: 8 minutes

Ingredients:
- 400g calamari rings
- 100g all-purpose flour
- 2 eggs, beaten
- 100g breadcrumbs
- 1/2 tsp paprika
- Salt and black pepper, to taste
- Cooking spray
- Fresh parsley, chopped (for garnish)
- For Aioli Dip:
- 150ml mayonnaise
- 1 clove garlic, minced
- Zest and juice of 1 lemon
- Salt and black pepper, to taste

Preparation instructions:
1. Preheat the Air Fryer to 200°C for 5 minutes.
2. In three separate bowls, place flour, beaten eggs, and a mixture of breadcrumbs, paprika, salt, and black pepper.
3. Dredge the calamari rings in flour, dip into the beaten eggs, then coat with the breadcrumb mixture, pressing gently to adhere.
4. Place the coated calamari rings in the Air Fryer basket, lightly spray with cooking spray. Air fry at 200°C for 8 minutes or until the calamari rings are crispy and golden brown, turning halfway through.
5. While the calamari is cooking, prepare the aioli dip by mixing mayonnaise, minced garlic, lemon zest, lemon juice, salt, and black pepper in a bowl.
6. Garnish the crispy calamari rings with chopped fresh parsley and serve with aioli dip.

Lemon Dill Air-Fried Cod Fillets

Serves: 4 / Prep time: 10 minutes / Cook time: 10 minutes

Ingredients:
- 4 cod fillets
- Zest and juice of 1 lemon
- 2 tbsp olive oil
- 2 cloves garlic, minced
- 1 tbsp fresh dill, chopped
- Salt and black pepper, to taste
- Lemon wedges, for serving

Preparation instructions:
1. Preheat the Air Fryer to 200°C for 5 minutes.
2. In a bowl, combine lemon zest, lemon juice, olive oil, minced garlic, fresh dill, salt, and black pepper.
3. Brush the cod fillets with the lemon dill mixture.
4. Place the cod fillets in the Air Fryer basket. Air fry at 200°C for 10 minutes or until the cod is cooked through and flakes easily with a fork.
5. Serve with lemon wedges.

Spicy Sriracha Salmon Burgers

Serves: 4 / Prep time: 15 minutes / Cook time: 10 minutes

Ingredients:
- 500g salmon fillet, skinless and boneless
- 2 tbsp Sriracha sauce
- 1 egg
- 50g breadcrumbs
- 2 green onions, finely chopped
- 1/2 tsp garlic powder

- Salt and black pepper, to taste
- 4 whole grain burger buns
- Lettuce leaves, tomato slices, and avocado slices (for assembling)

Preparation instructions:
1. Preheat the Air Fryer to 180°C for 5 minutes.
2. Cut the salmon fillet into chunks and place them in a food processor. Pulse until finely chopped.
3. In a bowl, combine chopped salmon, Sriracha sauce, egg, breadcrumbs, chopped green onions, garlic powder, salt, and black pepper. Mix well to form a thick mixture.
4. Divide the mixture into 4 portions and shape each portion into a burger patty.
5. Place the salmon patties in the Air Fryer basket. Air fry at 180°C for 10 minutes or until the salmon burgers are cooked through and golden brown, flipping halfway through the cooking time.
6. Toast the burger buns in the Air Fryer for 2 minutes.
7. Assemble the burgers by placing a salmon patty on the bottom half of each bun. Top with lettuce leaves, tomato slices, and avocado slices. Cover with the top half of the bun and serve immediately.

Crispy Fish Fingers with Tartar Sauce

Serves: 4 / Prep time: 15 minutes / Cook time: 10 minutes

Ingredients:
- 400g white fish fillets, cut into fingers
- 100g breadcrumbs
- 50g plain flour
- 2 eggs, beaten
- 1/2 tsp garlic powder
- 1/2 tsp paprika
- Salt and black pepper, to taste
- Cooking spray
- For Tartar Sauce:
- 150ml mayonnaise
- 2 tbsp gherkins, finely chopped
- 1 tbsp capers, chopped
- 1 tbsp fresh parsley, chopped
- 1/2 tsp Dijon mustard
- 1/2 lemon, juiced
- Salt and black pepper, to taste

Preparation instructions:
1. Preheat the Air Fryer to 190°C for 5 minutes.
2. In three separate bowls, place flour, beaten eggs mixed with garlic powder, paprika, salt, and black pepper, and breadcrumbs.
3. Dredge the fish fingers in flour, dip into the beaten eggs, then coat with breadcrumbs, pressing gently to adhere.
4. Place the coated fish fingers in the Air Fryer basket, lightly spray with cooking spray. Air fry at 190°C for 10 minutes or until the fish fingers are crispy and golden brown, turning halfway through.
5. While the fish fingers are cooking, prepare the tartar sauce by mixing mayonnaise, chopped gherkins, capers, fresh parsley, Dijon mustard, lemon juice, salt, and black pepper in a bowl.
6. Serve the crispy fish fingers with tartar sauce.

Garlic Butter Lobster Tails

Serves: 4 / Prep time: 10 minutes / Cook time: 10 minutes

Ingredients:
- 4 lobster tails, split in half
- 60g unsalted butter, melted
- 4 cloves garlic, minced
- 1 tbsp fresh parsley, chopped
- Salt and black pepper, to taste
- Lemon wedges, for serving

Preparation instructions:
1. Preheat the Air Fryer to 200°C for 5 minutes.
2. In a bowl, combine melted butter, minced garlic, fresh parsley, salt, and black pepper.
3. Brush the lobster tails with the garlic butter mixture.
4. Place the lobster tails in the Air Fryer basket, cut side up. Air fry at 200°C for 10 minutes or until the lobster is cooked through and opaque, basting with the remaining garlic

butter mixture halfway through.
5. Serve with lemon wedges.

Blackened Cajun Catfish Fillets

Serves: 4 / Prep time: 10 minutes / Cook time: 8 minutes

Ingredients:
- 4 catfish fillets
- 2 tbsp olive oil
- 1 tbsp Cajun seasoning
- 1/2 tsp paprika
- 1/2 tsp dried thyme
- 1/2 tsp garlic powder
- Salt and black pepper, to taste
- Fresh lemon wedges, for serving

Preparation instructions:
1. Preheat the Air Fryer to 200°C for 5 minutes.
2. In a bowl, combine olive oil, Cajun seasoning, paprika, dried thyme, garlic powder, salt, and black pepper.
3. Coat the catfish fillets evenly with the spice mixture.
4. Place the catfish fillets in the Air Fryer basket. Air fry at 200°C for 8 minutes or until the catfish is cooked through and flakes easily with a fork.
5. Serve with fresh lemon wedges.

Smoked Paprika Prawns with Aioli

Serves: 4 / Prep time: 10 minutes / Cook time: 6 minutes

Ingredients:
- 400g large prawns, peeled and deveined
- 2 tbsp olive oil
- 1 tsp smoked paprika
- 1/2 tsp garlic powder
- Salt and black pepper, to taste
- For Aioli:
- 150ml mayonnaise
- 1 clove garlic, minced
- 1/2 lemon, juiced
- Salt and black pepper, to taste

Preparation instructions:
1. Preheat the Air Fryer to 200°C for 5 minutes.
2. In a bowl, toss prawns with olive oil, smoked paprika, garlic powder, salt, and black pepper.
3. Place the seasoned prawns in the Air Fryer basket. Air fry at 200°C for 6 minutes or until the prawns are cooked through and lightly charred, shaking the basket halfway through.
4. While the prawns are cooking, prepare the aioli by mixing mayonnaise, minced garlic, lemon juice, salt, and black pepper in a bowl.
5. Serve the smoked paprika prawns with aioli.

Mediterranean Grilled Swordfish Steaks

Serves: 4 / Prep time: 15 minutes / Cook time: 10 minutes

Ingredients:
- 4 swordfish steaks
- 2 tbsp olive oil
- 1 tsp dried oregano
- 1/2 tsp dried basil
- 1/2 tsp garlic powder
- Salt and black pepper, to taste
- Fresh parsley, chopped (for garnish)
- Lemon wedges, for serving

Preparation instructions:
1. Preheat the Air Fryer to 200°C for 5 minutes.
2. In a bowl, combine olive oil, dried oregano, dried basil, garlic powder, salt, and black pepper.
3. Brush the swordfish steaks with the olive oil mixture.
4. Place the swordfish steaks in the Air Fryer basket. Air fry at 200°C for 10 minutes or until the swordfish is cooked through and flakes easily with a fork.
5. Garnish with chopped fresh parsley and serve with lemon wedges.

Chapter 9: Beef, Pork and Lamb Recipes

Succulent Air-Fried Beef Sirloin Steak

Serves: 4 / Prep time: 10 minutes / Cook time: 12 minutes

Ingredients:
- 4 beef sirloin steaks (about 150g each)
- 2 tbsp olive oil
- 1 tsp smoked paprika
- 1/2 tsp garlic powder
- 1/2 tsp onion powder
- Salt and black pepper, to taste
- Fresh parsley, chopped (for garnish)

Preparation instructions:
1. Preheat the Air Fryer to 200°C for 5 minutes.
2. In a bowl, combine olive oil, smoked paprika, garlic powder, onion powder, salt, and black pepper.
3. Brush both sides of the steaks with the spice mixture.
4. Place the steaks in the Air Fryer basket. Air fry at 200°C for 6 minutes for medium-rare, flipping halfway through, or adjust the time for desired doneness.
5. Remove the steaks from the Air Fryer and let them rest for a few minutes. Garnish with chopped fresh parsley before serving.

Crispy Pork Belly with Apple Compote

Serves: 4 / Prep time: 15 minutes / Cook time: 1 hour 10 minutes

Ingredients:
- 800g pork belly, skin on
- 1 tbsp olive oil
- 1 tsp smoked paprika
- 1/2 tsp dried thyme
- Salt and black pepper, to taste
- For Apple Compote:
- 2 apples, peeled, cored, and diced
- 2 tbsp unsalted butter
- 2 tbsp brown sugar
- 1/2 tsp ground cinnamon

Preparation instructions:
1. Preheat the Air Fryer to 200°C for 5 minutes.
2. Score the pork belly skin with a sharp knife, then rub olive oil, smoked paprika, dried thyme, salt, and black pepper all over the pork belly.
3. Place the pork belly in the Air Fryer basket, skin side up. Air fry at 200°C for 20 minutes.
4. Reduce the temperature to 180°C and continue air frying for 50 minutes or until the pork belly is crispy and cooked through.
5. While the pork belly is cooking, prepare the apple compote. In a saucepan, melt butter over medium heat. Add diced apples, brown sugar, and ground cinnamon. Cook until the apples are soft and caramelised, stirring occasionally.
6. Serve the crispy pork belly slices with the warm apple compote.

Spicy BBQ Pulled Pork Sliders

Serves: 4 / Prep time: 15 minutes / Cook time: 1 hour 15 minutes

Ingredients:
- 800g pork shoulder, trimmed of excess fat
- 1 onion, finely chopped
- 2 garlic cloves, minced
- 250ml BBQ sauce
- 1 tsp smoked paprika
- 1/2 tsp chilli powder
- 1/2 tsp cayenne pepper
- Salt and black pepper, to taste
- 4 small burger buns
- Coleslaw, for topping

Preparation instructions:
1. Preheat the Air Fryer to 160°C for 5 minutes.
2. In a bowl, combine chopped onion, minced garlic, BBQ sauce, smoked paprika, chilli powder, cayenne pepper, salt, and black

pepper.

3. Place the pork shoulder in the Air Fryer basket. Pour the BBQ sauce mixture over the pork.
4. Air fry at 160°C for 1 hour 15 minutes or until the pork is tender and can be easily shredded with a fork.
5. Remove the pork from the Air Fryer and shred it using two forks.
6. Toast the burger buns in the Air Fryer for 2-3 minutes.
7. Assemble the sliders by placing a generous amount of pulled pork on the bottom half of each bun. Top with coleslaw and the other half of the bun.

Air-Fried Lamb Chops with Mint Glaze

Serves: 4 / Prep time: 10 minutes / Cook time: 12 minutes

Ingredients:
- 8 lamb chops
- 2 tbsp olive oil
- 2 garlic cloves, minced
- 1 tsp dried rosemary
- Salt and black pepper, to taste
- For Mint Glaze:
- 2 tbsp fresh mint, finely chopped
- 2 tbsp honey
- 1 tbsp balsamic vinegar

Preparation instructions:
1. Preheat the Air Fryer to 200°C for 5 minutes.
2. In a bowl, combine olive oil, minced garlic, dried rosemary, salt, and black pepper. Rub the mixture over the lamb chops.
3. Place the lamb chops in the Air Fryer basket. Air fry at 200°C for 6 minutes for medium-rare, flipping halfway through, or adjust the time for desired doneness.
4. While the lamb chops are cooking, prepare the mint glaze by mixing fresh mint, honey, and balsamic vinegar in a bowl.
5. Brush the cooked lamb chops with the mint glaze before serving.

Classic Beef and Guinness Pie

Serves: 4 / Prep time: 20 minutes / Cook time: 1 hour 15 minutes

Ingredients:
- 500g beef stewing meat, cubed
- 1 onion, finely chopped
- 2 garlic cloves, minced
- 2 carrots, peeled and diced
- 200ml Guinness beer
- 250ml beef stock
- 2 tbsp tomato paste
- 1 tbsp Worcestershire sauce
- 1 tsp dried thyme
- Salt and black pepper, to taste
- 500g puff pastry
- 1 egg, beaten (for egg wash)

Preparation instructions:
1. Preheat the Air Fryer to 180°C for 5 minutes.
2. In a skillet, heat some olive oil over medium heat. Add cubed beef stewing meat and cook until browned on all sides. Remove the meat from the skillet and set aside.
3. In the same skillet, add chopped onion and minced garlic. Cook until translucent. Add diced carrots and cook for another 3-4 minutes.
4. Return the browned beef to the skillet. Pour in Guinness beer, beef stock, tomato paste, Worcestershire sauce, dried thyme, salt, and black pepper. Stir well. Simmer for 1 hour or until the beef is tender and the sauce has thickened.
5. Roll out the puff pastry on a floured surface and cut it into 4 circles, slightly larger than the size of your serving bowls.
6. Divide the beef filling among 4 oven-safe bowls. Place a puff pastry circle over each bowl, pressing the edges to seal. Brush the pastry with beaten egg.
7. Place the bowls in the Air Fryer basket. Air fry at 180°C for 15 minutes or until the pastry is golden and puffed up.
8. Serve the classic Beef and Guinness pies hot from the Air Fryer.

Sticky Teriyaki Pork Tenderloin

Serves: 4 / Prep time: 15 minutes / Cook time: 25 minutes

Ingredients:
- 500g pork tenderloin, sliced
- 60ml soy sauce
- 2 tbsp honey
- 2 tbsp mirin
- 1 garlic clove, minced
- 1 tsp grated fresh ginger
- 1 tbsp vegetable oil
- Sesame seeds and chopped green onions for garnish

Preparation instructions:
1. In a bowl, whisk together soy sauce, honey, mirin, minced garlic, and grated ginger to create the teriyaki sauce.
2. Marinate the pork tenderloin slices in half of the teriyaki sauce for at least 15 minutes.
3. Preheat the Air Fryer to 200°C for 5 minutes.
4. Heat vegetable oil in a pan over medium-high heat. Add marinated pork slices and cook until browned on both sides.
5. Place the cooked pork slices in one layer in the Air Fryer basket. Air fry at 200°C for 10-12 minutes, brushing with the remaining teriyaki sauce halfway through.
6. Garnish with sesame seeds and chopped green onions before serving.

Fragrant Rosemary Lamb Kebabs

Serves: 4 / Prep time: 20 minutes / Cook time: 15 minutes

Ingredients:
- 500g lamb, cubed
- 2 tbsp olive oil
- 2 tbsp fresh rosemary, chopped
- 2 garlic cloves, minced
- Salt and black pepper, to taste
- Lemon wedges for serving

Preparation instructions:
1. In a bowl, combine cubed lamb, olive oil, chopped rosemary, minced garlic, salt, and black pepper. Marinate for at least 15 minutes.
2. Preheat the Air Fryer to 200°C for 5 minutes.
3. Thread marinated lamb cubes onto skewers.
4. Place the lamb skewers in the Air Fryer basket. Air fry at 200°C for 12-15 minutes, turning halfway through, or until the lamb is cooked to your liking.
5. Serve with lemon wedges.

Air-Fried Beef Stir-Fry with Vegetables

Serves: 4 / Prep time: 15 minutes / Cook time: 10 minutes

Ingredients:
- 400g beef sirloin, thinly sliced
- 1 red bell pepper, sliced
- 1 yellow bell pepper, sliced
- 1 onion, sliced
- 2 tbsp soy sauce
- 1 tbsp oyster sauce
- 1 tbsp vegetable oil
- 1 garlic clove, minced
- 1 tsp grated fresh ginger
- Sesame seeds and chopped green onions for garnish

Preparation instructions:
1. In a bowl, mix together beef slices, soy sauce, and oyster sauce. Let it marinate for 10 minutes.
2. Preheat the Air Fryer to 200°C for 5 minutes.
3. Heat vegetable oil in a pan over medium-high heat. Add minced garlic and grated ginger, followed by marinated beef slices. Cook until the beef is browned. Add sliced bell peppers and onion, stir-frying for another 2-3 minutes until the vegetables are tender yet crisp.
4. Place the stir-fried beef and vegetables in the Air Fryer basket. Air fry at 200°C for 5 minutes.
5. Garnish with sesame seeds and chopped green onions before serving.

Tangy Balsamic Glazed Pork Ribs

Serves: 4 / Prep time: 20 minutes / Cook time: 35 minutes

Ingredients:
- 800g pork ribs
- Salt and black pepper, to taste
- 2 tbsp olive oil
- 80 ml balsamic vinegar
- 60ml honey
- 1 garlic clove, minced
- 1 tsp Dijon mustard
- Chopped fresh parsley for garnish

Preparation instructions:
1. Preheat the Air Fryer to 180°C for 5 minutes.
2. Season pork ribs with salt and black pepper.
3. Heat olive oil in a pan over medium-high heat. Add pork ribs and cook until browned on all sides. Remove excess oil from the pan.
4. In a small bowl, whisk together balsamic vinegar, honey, minced garlic, and Dijon mustard. Pour the mixture over the ribs in the pan. Simmer for a few minutes until the sauce thickens.
5. Place the glazed pork ribs in the Air Fryer basket. Air fry at 180°C for 30-35 minutes or until the ribs are cooked through and caramelised.
6. Garnish with chopped fresh parsley before serving.

Air-Fried Moroccan Lamb Meatballs

Serves: 4 / Prep time: 20 minutes / Cook time: 15 minutes

Ingredients:
- 500g ground lamb
- 1 small onion, finely chopped
- 2 garlic cloves, minced
- 1 tsp ground cumin
- 1 tsp ground coriander
- 1/2 tsp ground cinnamon
- Salt and black pepper, to taste
- 2 tbsp chopped fresh parsley
- 2 tbsp olive oil

Preparation instructions:
1. In a bowl, combine ground lamb, chopped onion, minced garlic, ground cumin, ground coriander, ground cinnamon, salt, black pepper, and chopped fresh parsley. Mix well and form the mixture into meatballs.
2. Preheat the Air Fryer to 180°C for 5 minutes.
3. Brush the meatballs with olive oil.
4. Place the meatballs in the Air Fryer basket. Air fry at 180°C for 12-15 minutes or until the meatballs are cooked through and browned on the outside.
5. Serve hot.

Crispy Pork Schnitzel with Lemon Butter

Serves: 4 / Prep time: 15 minutes / Cook time: 15 minutes

Ingredients:
- 4 pork loin chops, boneless, 150g each
- 100g all-purpose flour
- 2 large eggs, beaten
- 150g breadcrumbs
- Salt and black pepper, to taste
- Zest of 1 lemon
- 60g unsalted butter
- Fresh parsley, chopped, for garnish
- Lemon wedges, for serving

Preparation instructions:
1. Preheat the Air Fryer to 200°C for 5 minutes.
2. Season pork chops with salt, black pepper, and lemon zest.
3. Dredge each pork chop in flour, dip in beaten eggs, and coat with breadcrumbs, pressing gently to adhere.
4. Place the breaded pork chops in the Air Fryer basket. Air fry at 200°C for 15 minutes, turning halfway through, or until the pork is cooked through and crispy.
5. In a small saucepan, melt butter over low heat. Add a squeeze of lemon juice and stir well.
6. Drizzle the lemon butter over the crispy pork schnitzel.
7. Garnish with chopped fresh parsley and serve with lemon wedges.

Spicy Korean BBQ Beef Skewers

Serves: 4 / Prep time: 20 minutes / Cook time: 10 minutes

Ingredients:
- 500g beef sirloin, thinly sliced
- 4 tbsp gochujang (Korean red chilli paste)
- 2 tbsp soy sauce
- 2 tbsp honey
- 1 tbsp sesame oil
- 2 garlic cloves, minced
- 1 spring onion, finely chopped
- Sesame seeds, for garnish

Preparation instructions:
1. In a bowl, mix together gochujang, soy sauce, honey, sesame oil, minced garlic, and half of the chopped spring onion to make the marinade.
2. Marinate the thinly sliced beef in the mixture for at least 15 minutes.
3. Preheat the Air Fryer to 200°C for 5 minutes.
4. Thread marinated beef slices onto skewers.
5. Place the beef skewers in the Air Fryer basket. Air fry at 200°C for 8-10 minutes, turning occasionally, until the beef is cooked through.
6. Garnish with remaining chopped spring onion and sesame seeds before serving.

Air-Fried Garlic Rosemary Lamb Chops

Serves: 4 / Prep time: 15 minutes / Cook time: 12 minutes

Ingredients:
- 8 lamb loin chops, 150g each
- 3 tbsp olive oil
- 4 garlic cloves, minced
- 2 tbsp fresh rosemary, chopped
- Salt and black pepper, to taste
- Lemon wedges, for serving

Preparation instructions:
1. In a bowl, mix together olive oil, minced garlic, chopped rosemary, salt, and black pepper.
2. Rub the lamb chops with the garlic-rosemary mixture and let them marinate for at least 10 minutes.
3. Preheat the Air Fryer to 200°C for 5 minutes.
4. Place the marinated lamb chops in the Air Fryer basket. Air fry at 200°C for 12 minutes, turning halfway through, or until the lamb is cooked to your desired level of doneness.
5. Serve hot with lemon wedges.

Honey Mustard Glazed Pork Loin

Serves: 4 / Prep time: 10 minutes / Cook time: 25 minutes

Ingredients:
- 600g pork loin, boneless
- Salt and black pepper, to taste
- 4 tbsp honey
- 2 tbsp Dijon mustard
- 1 tbsp olive oil
- Fresh parsley, chopped, for garnish

Preparation instructions:
1. Preheat the Air Fryer to 200°C for 5 minutes.
2. Season pork loin with salt and black pepper.
3. In a small bowl, mix together honey and Dijon mustard to create the glaze.
4. Brush the pork loin with olive oil, then coat it evenly with the honey mustard glaze.
5. Place the pork loin in the Air Fryer basket. Air fry at 200°C for 25 minutes, turning halfway through, or until the pork is cooked through and caramelised.
6. Garnish with chopped fresh parsley before serving.

Fragrant Ginger Beef Stir Fry

Serves: 4 / Prep time: 20 minutes / Cook time: 10 minutes

Ingredients:
- 500g beef sirloin, thinly sliced
- 3 tbsp soy sauce
- 2 tbsp oyster sauce
- 1 tbsp honey
- 2 garlic cloves, minced
- 1 tbsp fresh ginger, grated
- 1 red bell pepper, sliced
- 1 yellow bell pepper, sliced
- 1 red onion, sliced
- 2 spring onions, sliced, for garnish
- Sesame seeds, for garnish

Preparation instructions:
1. In a bowl, mix together soy sauce, oyster

sauce, honey, minced garlic, and grated ginger to create the marinade.
2. Marinate the thinly sliced beef in the mixture for at least 15 minutes.
3. Preheat the Air Fryer to 200°C for 5 minutes.
4. In a separate bowl, toss the sliced bell peppers and red onion with a little olive oil.
5. Place the marinated beef and the vegetable mixture in the Air Fryer basket, ensuring an even layer.
6. Air fry at 200°C for 10 minutes, tossing halfway through, or until the beef is cooked and the vegetables are tender.
7. Garnish with sliced spring onions and sesame seeds before serving.

Savoury Lamb and Mushroom Pie

Serves: 4 / Prep time: 15 minutes / Cook time: 25 minutes

Ingredients:
- 400g lamb, diced
- 200g mushrooms, sliced
- 1 onion, finely chopped
- 2 cloves garlic, minced
- 2 tbsp olive oil
- 1 tsp dried thyme
- Salt and black pepper, to taste
- 300ml beef or vegetable stock
- 2 tbsp plain flour
- 1 sheet puff pastry, thawed if frozen

Preparation instructions:
1. Preheat the Air Fryer to 190°C for 5 minutes.
2. In a pan, heat olive oil over medium heat. Add diced lamb and cook until browned. Remove the lamb from the pan and set aside.
3. In the same pan, add onions, garlic, and mushrooms. Cook until the onions are translucent and mushrooms are tender.
4. Sprinkle flour over the mushroom mixture and stir well. Pour in the stock, stirring constantly until the mixture thickens.
5. Return the cooked lamb to the pan. Add dried thyme, salt, and black pepper. Stir to combine and let it simmer for a few minutes. Remove from heat and let it cool slightly.
6. Cut puff pastry into 4 squares or circles, depending on the shape of your pie dishes.
7. Divide the lamb and mushroom filling among the pie dishes. Cover each dish with a pastry square or circle, pressing the edges to seal.
8. Place the pies in the Air Fryer baskets. Air fry at 190°C for 25 minutes or until the pastry is golden and puffed.
9. Remove from the Air Fryer and let cool for a few minutes before serving.

Air-Fried Pork and Leek Dumplings

Serves: 4 / Prep time: 20 minutes / Cook time: 12 minutes

Ingredients:
- 300g pork mince
- 2 leeks, finely chopped
- 2 cloves garlic, minced
- 1 tbsp soy sauce
- 1 tsp sesame oil
- 1/2 tsp ground black pepper
- 1 pack dumpling wrappers (about 50 wrappers)

Preparation instructions:
1. In a bowl, mix together pork mince, chopped leeks, minced garlic, soy sauce, sesame oil, and black pepper.
2. Place a small spoonful of the pork mixture in the centre of each dumpling wrapper. Moisten the edges of the wrapper with water, then fold and seal the dumplings.
3. Preheat the Air Fryer to 180°C for 5 minutes.
4. Arrange the dumplings in the Air Fryer baskets in a single layer, making sure they are not touching.
5. Air fry at 180°C for 12 minutes or until the dumplings are golden and crispy.
6. Serve hot with soy sauce for dipping.

Beef and Mushroom Stuffed Peppers

Serves: 4 / Prep time: 15 minutes / Cook time: 20 minutes

Ingredients:
- 4 large bell peppers, any colour
- 300g beef mince
- 200g mushrooms, finely chopped
- 1 onion, finely chopped
- 2 cloves garlic, minced

- 1 tbsp olive oil
- 1 tsp dried oregano
- Salt and black pepper, to taste
- 200ml passata (strained tomatoes)

Preparation instructions:
1. Preheat the Air Fryer to 180°C for 5 minutes.
2. Cut the tops off the bell peppers and remove the seeds and membranes.
3. In a pan, heat olive oil over medium heat. Add onions, garlic, and mushrooms. Cook until the onions are translucent and mushrooms are tender.
4. Add beef mince to the pan. Cook until browned, breaking it up with a spoon as it cooks.
5. Season the mixture with dried oregano, salt, and black pepper. Stir in passata and cook for a few more minutes.
6. Stuff each bell pepper with the beef and mushroom mixture.
7. Place the stuffed peppers in the Air Fryer baskets. Air fry at 180°C for 20 minutes or until the peppers are tender.
8. Remove from the Air Fryer and let cool for a few minutes before serving.

Air-Fried Lamb Gyros with Tzatziki

Serves: 4 / Prep time: 20 minutes / Cook time: 12 minutes

Ingredients:
- 400g lamb leg or shoulder, thinly sliced
- 1 red onion, thinly sliced
- 2 tsp olive oil
- 1 tsp ground cumin
- 1 tsp ground coriander
- Salt and black pepper, to taste
- 4 pitta breads, warmed
- Fresh parsley, chopped, for garnish
- Tzatziki:
- 150g Greek yoghurt
- 1/2 cucumber, grated and drained
- 1 clove garlic, minced
- 1 tbsp lemon juice
- Salt and black pepper, to taste

Preparation instructions:
1. Preheat the Air Fryer to 200°C for 5 minutes.
2. In a bowl, mix sliced lamb with olive oil, ground cumin, ground coriander, salt, and black pepper.
3. Place the marinated lamb slices and sliced red onion in the Air Fryer basket. Air fry at 200°C for 12 minutes or until the lamb is cooked through.
4. While the lamb is cooking, prepare the tzatziki by combining Greek yoghurt, grated and drained cucumber, minced garlic, lemon juice, salt, and black pepper.
5. Warm the pitta breads in the Air Fryer for 1-2 minutes.
6. Assemble gyros by placing cooked lamb and red onion on warm pitta breads. Top with tzatziki and chopped fresh parsley.
7. Serve immediately.

Pork and Sage Sausage Rolls

Serves: 4 / Prep time: 15 minutes / Cook time: 15 minutes

Ingredients:
- 400g pork sausages, casings removed
- 1 tbsp fresh sage, chopped
- 1 sheet puff pastry, thawed if frozen
- 1 egg, beaten, for egg wash
- Sesame seeds, for garnish

Preparation instructions:
1. Preheat the Air Fryer to 200°C for 5 minutes.
2. In a bowl, combine pork sausages with chopped sage, mixing well.
3. Roll out the puff pastry sheet and cut it in half lengthwise.
4. Divide the sausage mixture into two portions and shape each portion into a log along the length of each pastry half.
5. Roll the pastry around the sausage filling and seal the edges. Cut each roll into smaller rolls.
6. Brush the rolls with beaten egg and sprinkle sesame seeds on top.
7. Place the rolls in the Air Fryer baskets. Air fry at 200°C for 15 minutes or until the rolls are golden and crispy.
8. Remove from the Air Fryer and let cool for a few minutes before serving.

Chapter 10: Sweet Treats and Dessert Recipes

Air-Fried Apple Fritters with Cinnamon Sugar

Serves: 4 / Prep time: 15 minutes / Cook time: 12 minutes

Ingredients:
- 200g all-purpose flour
- 2 tbsp granulated sugar
- 1 tsp baking powder
- 1/2 tsp ground cinnamon
- 1/4 tsp salt
- 120ml whole milk
- 2 apples, peeled, cored, and chopped into small pieces
- Vegetable oil, for frying
- 50g granulated sugar, for coating
- 1 tsp ground cinnamon, for coating

Preparation instructions:
1. In a bowl, combine the flour, sugar, baking powder, ground cinnamon, and salt.
2. Gradually add the milk, stirring until a thick batter forms.
3. Fold in the chopped apples until evenly distributed in the batter.
4. Preheat the Air Fryer to 180°C for 5 minutes.
5. Drop spoonfuls of the batter into the Air Fryer basket, ensuring they are not touching.
6. Air fry at 180°C for 12 minutes or until the fritters are golden brown and cooked through.
7. While the fritters are cooking, mix the remaining sugar and ground cinnamon in a bowl for coating.
8. As soon as the fritters are done, roll them in the cinnamon sugar mixture to coat evenly.
9. Serve the apple fritters warm.

Crispy Mini Jam Doughnuts

Serves: 4 / Prep time: 15 minutes / Cook time: 10 minutes

Ingredients:
- 200g all-purpose flour
- 2 tbsp granulated sugar
- 1 tsp baking powder
- 1/4 tsp salt
- 120ml whole milk
- 2 tbsp strawberry jam
- Vegetable oil, for frying
- 50g icing sugar, for dusting

Preparation instructions:
1. In a bowl, combine the flour, sugar, baking powder, and salt.
2. Gradually add the milk, stirring until a thick batter forms.
3. Preheat the Air Fryer to 180°C for 5 minutes.
4. Spoon a small amount of batter into the palm of your hand. Place a small amount of jam in the centre and encase it with batter, forming a small ball.
5. Drop the doughnut balls into the Air Fryer basket, ensuring they are not touching.
6. Air fry at 180°C for 10 minutes or until the doughnuts are golden brown and cooked through.
7. While the doughnuts are cooking, sift the icing sugar into a bowl.
8. As soon as the doughnuts are done, roll them in the icing sugar to coat evenly.
9. Serve the mini jam doughnuts warm.

Decadent Chocolate Lava Cake

Serves: 4 / Prep time: 10 minutes / Cook time: 12 minutes

Ingredients:
- 100g dark chocolate, chopped
- 100g unsalted butter
- 2 large eggs
- 2 egg yolks
- 50g granulated sugar
- 30g all-purpose flour
- Cocoa powder, for dusting
- Vanilla ice cream, for serving (optional)

Preparation instructions:
1. Preheat the Air Fryer to 180°C for 5 minutes.

2. In a microwave-safe bowl, melt the dark chocolate and butter together. Stir until smooth and let it cool slightly.
3. In another bowl, whisk the eggs, egg yolks, and sugar until pale and fluffy.
4. Gradually fold the melted chocolate mixture into the egg mixture.
5. Sift in the flour and gently fold until well combined.
6. Grease four ramekins and pour the batter evenly into them.
7. Place the ramekins in the Air Fryer basket. Air fry at 180°C for 12 minutes or until the cakes are set around the edges but still soft in the centre.
8. Remove from the Air Fryer and let cool for a minute. Run a knife around the edges and invert the cakes onto plates.
9. Dust with cocoa powder and serve with vanilla ice cream, if desired.

Sticky Toffee Pudding Bites

Serves: 4 / Prep time: 15 minutes / Cook time: 10 minutes

Ingredients:
- 150g dates, pitted and chopped
- 180ml boiling water
- 1 tsp vanilla extract
- 80g unsalted butter, softened
- 150g brown sugar
- 2 large eggs
- 180g self-raising flour
- 1/2 tsp baking soda
- 100ml double cream
- 50g dark chocolate, chopped

Preparation instructions:
1. Preheat the Air Fryer to 180°C for 5 minutes.
2. In a bowl, combine the dates, boiling water, and vanilla extract. Let it sit for 10 minutes.
3. In another bowl, cream the softened butter and brown sugar until light and fluffy.
4. Beat in the eggs, one at a time, until well incorporated.
5. Sift in the self-raising flour and baking soda. Mix until just combined.
6. Fold in the soaked dates.
7. Grease a mini muffin tin and spoon the batter into the cups.
8. Air fry at 180°C for 10 minutes or until a toothpick inserted into the centre comes out clean.
9. While the pudding bites are cooking, heat the double cream in a pan until it starts to simmer. Remove from heat and stir in the chopped dark chocolate until smooth.
10. Serve the warm sticky toffee pudding bites drizzled with the chocolate sauce.

Banana Bread

Serves: 8 / Prep time: 15 minutes / Cook time: 40 minutes

Ingredients:
- 250g ripe bananas, mashed
- 200g all-purpose flour
- 100g granulated sugar
- 60ml vegetable oil
- 60ml whole milk
- 2 large eggs
- 1 tsp baking powder
- 1/2 tsp baking soda
- 1/4 tsp salt
- 1/2 tsp ground cinnamon
- 1/4 tsp ground nutmeg
- 1 tsp vanilla extract

Preparation instructions:
1. Preheat the Air Fryer to 180°C for 5 minutes.
2. In a large bowl, whisk together the mashed bananas, sugar, vegetable oil, whole milk, and eggs until well combined.
3. In another bowl, sift together the all-purpose flour, baking powder, baking soda, salt, ground cinnamon, and ground nutmeg.
4. Gradually add the dry ingredients to the wet ingredients, mixing until just combined. Do not overmix.
5. Stir in the vanilla extract.
6. Grease a loaf pan that fits inside the Air Fryer basket.
7. Pour the banana bread batter into the prepared loaf pan.

8. Place the loaf pan in the Air Fryer basket and air fry at 180°C for 40 minutes or until a toothpick inserted into the centre of the bread comes out clean.
9. Once cooked, remove the banana bread from the Air Fryer and let it cool in the pan for 10 minutes.
10. Transfer the banana bread to a wire rack to cool completely before slicing and serving.

Classic Victoria Sponge Cake

Serves: 8 / Prep time: 15 minutes / Cook time: 25 minutes

Ingredients:
- 200g unsalted butter, softened
- 200g caster sugar
- 4 large eggs
- 200g self-raising flour
- 1 tsp baking powder
- 2 tbsp whole milk
- 1 tsp vanilla extract
- 150g raspberry jam
- 150ml double cream
- Icing sugar, for dusting

Preparation instructions:
1. Preheat the Air Fryer to 160°C for 5 minutes.
2. In a large bowl, cream together the softened butter and caster sugar until light and fluffy.
3. Beat in the eggs, one at a time, and add the vanilla extract.
4. Sift the self-raising flour and baking powder into the wet ingredients. Fold gently until well combined.
5. Add the whole milk and mix until the batter is smooth and creamy.
6. Grease two 20cm round cake tins and divide the batter evenly between them.
7. Place the cake tins in the Air Fryer baskets. Air fry at 160°C for 25 minutes or until a skewer inserted into the centre comes out clean.
8. Remove the cakes from the Air Fryer and let them cool completely on a wire rack.
9. Once the cakes are cool, spread raspberry jam on top of one cake layer.
10. Whip the double cream until it forms soft peaks. Spread the whipped cream over the jam.
11. Place the second cake layer on top.
12. Dust the top of the cake with icing sugar before serving.

Zesty Lemon Curd Tarts

Makes: 6 tarts / Prep time: 20 minutes / Cook time: 15 minutes

Ingredients:
- 1 sheet ready-rolled shortcrust pastry (about 320g)
- 200g lemon curd
- 1 lemon, zested
- Icing sugar, for dusting
- Fresh raspberries and mint leaves, for garnish

Preparation instructions:
1. Preheat the Air Fryer to 180°C for 5 minutes.
2. Using a round cutter, cut out 6 circles from the pastry sheet to fit your tart tins.
3. Press the pastry circles into the tart tins, ensuring the edges are neat.
4. Prick the base of each tart with a fork, then spoon 1 to 2 tablespoons of lemon curd into each tart shell.
5. Air fry the tarts at 180°C for 15 minutes or until the pastry is golden brown and the lemon curd is set.
6. Remove the tarts from the Air Fryer and let them cool slightly.
7. Sprinkle lemon zest over the tarts and dust with icing sugar.
8. Garnish with fresh raspberries and mint leaves before serving.

Air-Fried Raspberry Cheesecake Bites

Makes: 12 bites / Prep time: 15 minutes / Cook time: 12 minutes

Ingredients:
- 200g cream cheese, softened
- 50g caster sugar
- 1 egg

- 1/2 tsp vanilla extract
- 6 digestive biscuits, crushed into fine crumbs
- 50g fresh raspberries

Preparation instructions:
1. Preheat the Air Fryer to 160°C for 5 minutes.
2. In a bowl, beat the cream cheese and caster sugar until smooth and creamy.
3. Add the egg and vanilla extract, and beat until well combined.
4. Fold in the crushed digestive biscuits and fresh raspberries.
5. Using a spoon, drop heaping tablespoons of the cheesecake mixture onto a parchment-lined tray, forming 12 individual bites.
6. Air fry the cheesecake bites at 160°C for 12 minutes or until they are set and lightly golden on top.
7. Remove the cheesecake bites from the Air Fryer and let them cool completely before serving.

Cinnamon Sugar Churros with Chocolate Sauce

Serves: 4 / Prep time: 15 minutes / Cook time: 10 minutes

Ingredients:
- 200g plain flour
- 1/2 tsp baking powder
- 1/2 tsp salt
- 1 tbsp vegetable oil
- 250ml boiling water
- Vegetable oil, for frying
- 100g caster sugar
- 1 tsp ground cinnamon
- 100g dark chocolate, chopped
- 100ml double cream

Preparation instructions:
1. In a mixing bowl, combine plain flour, baking powder, and salt.
2. Add 1 tablespoon of vegetable oil and boiling water to the dry ingredients. Stir until a dough forms.
3. Transfer the dough to a piping bag fitted with a star-shaped nozzle.
4. Preheat your Air Fryer to 180°C (356°F) for 5 minutes.
5. Pipe strips of dough directly into the Air Fryer basket, cutting them with scissors. Leave space between churros for even cooking.
6. Air fry the churros at 180°C (356°F) for 8-10 minutes, or until they are golden brown and crispy, turning them halfway through the cooking time for even cooking.
7. In a separate bowl, mix caster sugar and ground cinnamon.
8. Once the churros are cooked, remove them from the Air Fryer and immediately roll them in the cinnamon sugar mixture to coat them evenly.
9. In a small saucepan, heat double cream until hot but not boiling. Remove from heat and add the chopped dark chocolate. Stir until smooth to make the chocolate sauce.
10. Serve the warm churros with the chocolate sauce for dipping. Enjoy your delicious homemade churros made effortlessly in the Air Fryer!

Blueberry and Cream Cheese Air-Fried Pastry

Serves: 4 / Prep time: 20 minutes / Cook time: 12 minutes

Ingredients:
- 1 sheet puff pastry (about 320g), thawed if frozen
- 100g cream cheese, softened
- 2 tbsp icing sugar
- 1/2 tsp vanilla extract
- 100g fresh blueberries
- Icing sugar, for dusting

Preparation instructions:
1. Preheat the Air Fryer to 180°C for 5 minutes.
2. Roll out the puff pastry sheet on a lightly floured surface. Cut it into 4 equal squares.
3. In a bowl, mix together the softened cream cheese, icing sugar, and vanilla extract until smooth.
4. Spread a dollop of the cream cheese mixture in the centre of each pastry square.

5. Scatter fresh blueberries over the cream cheese layer.
6. Fold the pastry squares diagonally to form triangles, pressing the edges to seal.
7. Place the pastries in the Air Fryer basket. Air fry at 180°C for 12 minutes or until the pastries are puffed and golden brown.
8. Remove the pastries from the Air Fryer and let them cool slightly.
9. Dust with icing sugar before serving.

Crispy Custard-Filled Eclairs

Serves: 4 / Prep time: 20 minutes / Cook time: 20 minutes

Ingredients:
- 150ml water
- 75g unsalted butter
- 1/4 tsp salt
- 90g plain flour
- 3 large eggs
- 500ml whole milk
- 4 tbsp caster sugar
- 2 tbsp cornflour
- 1 tsp vanilla extract
- Icing sugar, for dusting

Preparation instructions:
1. Preheat the Air Fryer to 190°C for 5 minutes.
2. In a saucepan, combine water, butter, and salt. Heat until the butter is melted and the mixture comes to a boil.
3. Reduce heat to low, add flour all at once, and stir vigorously until the mixture forms a ball. Remove from heat and let it cool for 5 minutes.
4. Beat in the eggs, one at a time, ensuring each egg is fully incorporated before adding the next.
5. Transfer the mixture to a piping bag fitted with a large round nozzle. Pipe 10 cm long strips onto a parchment-lined tray.
6. Air fry the eclairs at 190°C for 20 minutes or until golden brown and puffed. Remove from the Air Fryer and let them cool.
7. For the custard filling, in a saucepan, whisk together milk, caster sugar, cornflour, and vanilla extract. Cook over medium heat, stirring constantly until the mixture thickens.
8. Once thickened, remove from heat and let it cool completely.
9. Cut the cooled eclairs horizontally and fill them with the custard.
10. Dust with icing sugar before serving.

Air-Fried Sticky Caramel Pudding

Serves: 4 / Prep time: 15 minutes / Cook time: 20 minutes

Ingredients:
- 100g self-raising flour
- 1/2 tsp baking powder
- 50g unsalted butter, softened
- 50g caster sugar
- 1 large egg
- 2 tbsp milk
- 100g soft caramels, chopped
- 150ml double cream
- 1 tbsp golden syrup

Preparation instructions:
1. Preheat the Air Fryer to 180°C for 5 minutes.
2. In a bowl, sift together self-raising flour and baking powder.
3. In another bowl, cream together softened butter and caster sugar until light and fluffy.
4. Beat in the egg and gradually add the sifted flour mixture, alternating with milk, until well combined.
5. Grease 4 individual pudding moulds and place chopped soft caramels at the bottom of each mould.
6. Spoon the cake batter over the caramels in each mould.
7. In a saucepan, heat double cream and golden syrup until hot but not boiling. Pour this sauce over the cake batter in the moulds.
8. Air fry the puddings at 180°C for 20 minutes or until the puddings are cooked through and golden brown.
9. Let the puddings cool for a few minutes before serving. Invert them onto plates to serve, allowing the caramel sauce to drizzle over the top.

Raspberry and Almond Frangipane Tartlets

Serves: 4 / Prep time: 20 minutes / Cook time: 25 minutes

Ingredients:
- 1 sheet ready-rolled shortcrust pastry (about 320g)
- 75g unsalted butter, softened
- 75g caster sugar
- 1 large egg
- 75g ground almonds
- 1/2 tsp almond extract
- 100g fresh raspberries
- Icing sugar, for dusting

Preparation instructions:
1. Preheat the Air Fryer to 180°C for 5 minutes.
2. Using a round cutter, cut out 4 circles from the pastry sheet to fit your tartlet tins.
3. Press the pastry circles into the tartlet tins, ensuring the edges are neat. Prick the bases with a fork.
4. In a bowl, cream together softened butter and caster sugar until light and fluffy.
5. Beat in the egg and almond extract, then fold in the ground almonds.
6. Spread the almond mixture evenly over the pastry in each tartlet tin.
7. Press fresh raspberries gently into the almond mixture.
8. Air fry the tartlets at 180°C for 25 minutes or until the pastry is golden brown and the almond filling is set.
9. Remove the tartlets from the Air Fryer and let them cool slightly. Dust with icing sugar before serving.

Air-Fried Mango Coconut Spring Rolls

Serves: 4 / Prep time: 15 minutes / Cook time: 10 minutes

Ingredients:
- 4 spring roll wrappers
- 1 ripe mango, peeled, pitted, and thinly sliced
- 50g shredded coconut, toasted
- 2 tbsp honey
- 1 tbsp butter, melted
- Vanilla ice cream, for serving

Preparation instructions:
1. Preheat the Air Fryer to 180°C for 5 minutes.
2. Place a spring roll wrapper on a clean surface. Arrange mango slices and toasted shredded coconut in the centre of the wrapper.
3. Drizzle honey over the mango and coconut. Roll up the wrapper, folding in the sides, to create a spring roll. Seal the edge with a little melted butter.
4. Repeat with the remaining wrappers and filling.
5. Place the spring rolls in the Air Fryer basket. Air fry at 180°C for 10 minutes or until the spring rolls are crispy and golden brown.
6. Serve the spring rolls warm with a scoop of vanilla ice cream.

Mini Pavlovas with Fresh Berries

Serves: 4 / Prep time: 15 minutes / Cook time: 1 hour

Ingredients:
- 2 large egg whites
- 100g caster sugar
- 1/2 tsp white vinegar
- 1/2 tsp vanilla extract
- 150ml double cream
- Fresh mixed berries (such as strawberries, blueberries, raspberries) for topping

Preparation instructions:
1. Preheat the Air Fryer to 120°C for 5 minutes.
2. In a clean, dry bowl, beat the egg whites until soft peaks form.
3. Gradually add the caster sugar, one tablespoon at a time, beating well after each addition, until the mixture is glossy and stiff peaks form.
4. Beat in the white vinegar and vanilla extract.
5. Spoon the meringue mixture into 4 individual portions on a parchment-lined tray

in the Air Fryer basket.
6. Create a well in the centre of each meringue to hold the toppings.
7. Air fry the meringues at 120°C for 1 hour or until they are crisp on the outside and soft on the inside. Allow them to cool completely.
8. In the meantime, whip the double cream until soft peaks form.
9. Once the meringues are cool, fill the wells with the whipped cream and top with fresh mixed berries.
10. Serve the mini pavlovas immediately. Enjoy your delightful dessert!

Air-Fried Chocolate Orange Profiteroles

Serves: 4 / Prep time: 15 minutes / Cook time: 20 minutes

Ingredients:
- 100g plain flour
- 80 ml water
- 60g unsalted butter
- 2 large eggs
- 300ml double cream
- Zest of 1 orange
- 100g dark chocolate, chopped
- 60ml whole milk
- 1 tbsp icing sugar, for dusting

Preparation instructions:
1. Preheat the Air Fryer to 200°C for 5 minutes.
2. In a saucepan, combine water and butter over medium heat until the butter melts. Bring to a boil, remove from heat, and quickly stir in the flour until a smooth dough forms.
3. Allow the dough to cool slightly, then beat in the eggs one at a time, mixing well after each addition. The mixture should be smooth and glossy.
4. Transfer the dough to a piping bag and pipe small mounds onto a parchment-lined tray. Air fry at 200°C for 15-18 minutes or until golden and puffed. Allow to cool.
5. In a separate bowl, whip the double cream until soft peaks form. Fold in the orange zest gently.
6. In a heatproof bowl, melt the dark chocolate and milk together in the Air Fryer at 160°C for 5 minutes, stirring occasionally until smooth.
7. Cut the cooled profiteroles in half horizontally. Fill each profiterole with whipped cream and drizzle with the chocolate sauce.
8. Dust with icing sugar before serving. Enjoy your delightful chocolate orange profiteroles!

Spiced Apple and Walnut Turnovers

Serves: 4 / Prep time: 20 minutes / Cook time: 15 minutes

Ingredients:
- 2 apples, peeled, cored, and diced
- 50g chopped walnuts
- 2 tbsp brown sugar
- 1/2 tsp ground cinnamon
- 1/4 tsp ground nutmeg
- 1 sheet puff pastry, thawed
- 1 egg, beaten
- Icing sugar, for dusting

Preparation instructions:
1. Preheat the Air Fryer to 180°C for 5 minutes.
2. In a bowl, mix together diced apples, walnuts, brown sugar, ground cinnamon, and ground nutmeg.
3. Roll out the puff pastry sheet and cut it into 4 squares.
4. Place a spoonful of the apple-walnut mixture in the centre of each pastry square. Fold the pastry over the filling to create a turnover, pressing the edges to seal.
5. Brush the turnovers with beaten egg and place them in the Air Fryer basket.
6. Air fry at 180°C for 12-15 minutes or until the turnovers are golden and crispy.
7. Dust with icing sugar before serving. Enjoy your spiced apple and walnut turnovers!

Air-Fried Chocolate Hazelnut Calzones

Serves: 4 / Prep time: 20 minutes / Cook time:

15 minutes

Ingredients:
- 1 sheet pizza dough
- 100g chocolate hazelnut spread
- 1 banana, sliced
- 1 tbsp chopped hazelnuts
- Icing sugar, for dusting

Preparation instructions:
1. Preheat the Air Fryer to 180°C for 5 minutes.
2. Roll out the pizza dough and cut it into 4 equal squares.
3. Spread a generous spoonful of chocolate hazelnut spread on one half of each square. Top with banana slices and chopped hazelnuts.
4. Fold the other half of the dough over the filling to create a calzone, pressing the edges to seal.
5. Place the calzones in the Air Fryer basket.
6. Air fry at 180°C for 12-15 minutes or until the calzones are golden and crispy.
7. Dust with icing sugar before serving. Enjoy your chocolate hazelnut calzones!

Black Forest Cherry and Chocolate Parfait

Serves: 4 / Prep time: 15 minutes / Chill time: 1 hour

Ingredients:
- 200g cherries, pitted and halved
- 2 tbsp sugar
- 300ml double cream
- 100g dark chocolate, chopped
- 1 tsp vanilla extract
- 50g chocolate shavings, for garnish

Preparation instructions:
1. In a saucepan, combine cherries and sugar. Cook over medium heat until the cherries release their juices and become tender. Remove from heat and let cool.
2. In a heatproof bowl, melt the dark chocolate in the Air Fryer at 160°C for 5 minutes, stirring occasionally until smooth. Let it cool slightly.
3. In a separate bowl, whip the double cream and vanilla extract until soft peaks form.
4. Layer the parfait glasses with whipped cream, cherries, and melted chocolate, repeating the layers until the glasses are filled.
5. Refrigerate the parfaits for at least 1 hour to set.
6. Before serving, garnish with chocolate shavings. Enjoy your black forest cherry and chocolate parfait!

Crispy Air-Fried Pineapple Fritters

Serves: 4 / Prep time: 15 minutes / Cook time: 10 minutes

Ingredients:
- 1 ripe pineapple, peeled, cored, and cut into rings
- 150g plain flour
- 2 tbsp cornstarch
- 1/2 tsp baking powder
- 1/4 tsp salt
- 1/2 tsp ground cinnamon
- 1/4 tsp ground nutmeg
- 180ml cold water
- Vegetable oil, for frying
- Icing sugar, for dusting

Preparation instructions:
1. Preheat the Air Fryer to 180°C for 5 minutes.
2. In a bowl, whisk together flour, cornstarch, baking powder, salt, ground cinnamon, and ground nutmeg. Gradually add cold water, whisking until the batter is smooth.
3. Dip each pineapple ring into the batter, ensuring it's fully coated.
4. Heat vegetable oil in a pan over medium heat. Fry the battered pineapple rings until golden brown on both sides. Drain on paper towels.
5. Place the fried pineapple rings in the Air Fryer basket. Air fry at 180°C for 5-7 minutes or until crispy.
6. Dust with icing sugar before serving. Enjoy your crispy air-fried pineapple fritters!

Printed in Great Britain
by Amazon